Learning
Grace

finding God in failure

Copyright 2019
Michael M. Middleton

All Scriptures NKJV

copyright 1984, Thomas Nelson, Inc
Used by permission.

<u>Ancient of Days</u>

Above all, beyond all---
the All in all
and more…

O Ancient of Days, eternal source,
to You alone
my praises soar.

Neither the highest of heavens,
nor the deepest sea
in fiercest desire
could ever aspire
to contain Thee.

You spoke,
and it was;
creation came to be…

You loved
beyond measure
and set this captive free.

Michael M. Middleton

Introduction

"Out of the depths I have cried to You, O Lord; Lord, hear my voice! Let Your ears be attentive to the voice of my supplications. If You, Lord, should mark iniquities, O Lord, who could stand? But there is forgiveness with You, that You may be feared. I wait for the Lord, my soul waits, and in His word I do hope. My soul waits for the Lord more than those who watch for the morning — yes, more than those who watch for the morning. O Israel, hope in the Lord, for with the Lord there is mercy, and with Him is abundant redemption. And He shall redeem Israel from all his iniquities." Psalm 130

The book you now hold in your hands was, in many respects, born of failure. I have lived on this little blue and green planet for quite nearly five decades as of this writing. For better than four of those decades, I have been in serious pursuit of my Creator. For the past three decades, I have been privileged to train and serve in full time ministry, primarily through Youth With A Mission. Unfortunately, if you were to assume that someone who has lived such a life must certainly have it all together spiritually, you would be tragically wrong.

I have spent far too many of my days living on the

dark side of Romans chapter 7...doing things I know I shouldn't do — and becoming intimately familiar with the shackles of regret. The Lord has gifted me in the area of the prophetic, both in terms of spiritual gifting and as a framework to my personality. While there have been many wonderful blessings associated with this — some of which I will discuss later — there is also a substantial burden attached to this gifting. If one's prophetic anointing is truly of the Lord, they will find themselves being hardest of all on their own shortcomings. We tend to internalize our failures quite deeply, and the "silent prophet" is one who is too busy yelling at themselves on the inside to say much to others on the outside. Though we often have difficulty verbalizing it, yes...yes, we know when we have blown it.

While wallowing in a particular bout of such frustration and regret some years ago, I let slip a heartfelt question to the Lord: **"How long are you willing to keep putting up with me — doing the same stupid thing over and over?!?"** Immediately as the words flew off of my lips, I realized that I was not asking a rhetorical question; my spirit held a spark of anticipation, expecting an answer.

That answer came quickly. In one of the rare instances where I have heard the Lord speak audibly, His reply came gently to my ears and sank swiftly to the depths of my heart:

"As long as you are willing to keep trying..."

This reply surprised me, shocked me... It was not at all in line with what I would expect to hear — what I knew at that moment that I deserved to hear. Perhaps God was not ready to discard me yet. Perhaps He was not as frustrated with me as I was with myself. Perhaps there was more to His patience, compassion, and longsuffering than I had estimated. Perhaps He was more on my side than I had believed.

This moment of realization became a landmark of change for me. I began to ask God not *just* for forgiveness, which was already accomplished, but for strategies to overcome. I began to ask God to redeem my shortcomings and to use the times when I fell short to <u>teach me</u> something of Himself... to rescue out of the darkness some new revelation of light.

To **redeem** means to rescue, to buy back, to get good out of a bad situation. Our sins and shortcomings are never God's plan or desire, but He is capable, as His word says, of working ALL things together for good. (See Romans 8:28) That does not mean that *all things* are part of His original plan or design — sin is still sin and still wrong. It does, however, mean that He can work with anything laid upon His altar to bring good out of it in the end…and delights in doing so. Redemption is one of the central aspects of His nature.

Bearing this in mind, this book is dedicated primarily to two groups of people. The first group would be those like myself who consider themselves Christians, but find themselves too often weighed down and discouraged by their own shortcomings. *There is hope.* Freedom and victory lies in exploring the unfathomable depths of God's love, which no man can exhaust.

The not yet committed but honest seeker may find great value in this work as well. It may just help to correct some popular misconceptions about what it means to be a follower of Jesus and help to open your eyes to just how amazing *Amazing Grace* truly is. If you do find yourself among this second group, I commend you for being open enough to read this far. Before getting into some of the deeper things contained herein, however, I would suggest that you get a "bottom line" perspective by turning to *The Dirt Simple Bible* near the end of this book. This is a short teaching article I wrote many years ago while serving as a youth minister and pioneering an inner city youth drop-in center with The Salvation Army.

For both of the above mentioned groups of people, know this: the Lord of Glory is for you. No matter what your past may be, it can be swallowed up in a glorious future. All that is required is a willing heart.

"The Spirit of the Lord God is upon Me, because the Lord has anointed Me to preach good tidings to the poor; He has sent Me to heal the brokenhearted, proclaim liberty to the captives, and the opening of the prison to those who are bound; to proclaim the acceptable year of the Lord, and the day of vengeance of our God; to comfort all who mourn, to console those who mourn in Zion, to give them beauty for ashes, the oil of joy for mourning, the garment of praise for the spirit of heaviness; that they may be called trees of righteousness, the planting of the Lord, that He may be glorified." Isaiah 61:1-3

Of two minds...

Realizing a fuller understanding of Scripture and of the divine Author thereof is no weekend task. As we will discuss in somewhat greater detail later, it is indeed much more than a life-long project — immeasurably more. Coming to really know and understand our Maker is a process which will continue throughout the endless ages of eternity. After all, when infinity is your goal, you will never truly arrive — and yet there is such tremendous joy in the journey.

In some sense, those of us in the western world are innately handicapped in our understanding of Scripture. We have grown up in and are saturated by a western, analytical mindset. While there _is_ great strength and benefit in this, if one leans solely upon a dry, cold intellect, they will never truly understand the living God. He is not an office copy machine or an internet server. He is a living being — with both intellect _and_ emotion, thought _and_ will far beyond our minute capacity. You cannot simply approach Him like you would a troubleshooting manual on computer repair. To really begin to KNOW Him, you must also seek to experience His being at a heart level.

To really begin to know God, you must become a

man or woman of two minds. Scripture was primarily originally authored in two languages, Hebrew and Greek. In large measure, the portions of Scripture written in each tongue strongly reflect in both style and content the cultures and mindsets of their human authors and original audiences. Let us briefly discuss these two mindsets and how they, taken in balance, contribute to a much fuller understanding of the one true God.

The Greek Mindset

We will begin with what is most familiar to the majority of those who will read this book — the Greek or "western" mindset. You may also wish to refer to this as the *left-brained* approach. The left side of your brain is believed to be the center of the intellect, as expressed in the function of linear, analytical thought. This gives a pretty accurate picture overall of the culture to which much of the New Testament was originally penned. It goes something like this:

"It walks like a duck. It talks like a duck. Ladies and gentlemen of the jury, inarguably... it is therefore a duck. The prosecution rests, your honor."

Now, there is certainly nothing wrong with this mental viewpoint playing a role in how we approach the study of Scripture. As Paul exhorts in 2 Timothy 2:15, *"Be diligent to present yourself approved to God, a worker who does not need to be ashamed, rightly dividing the word of truth."* (The original King James version renders this, *"***Study*** to shew thyself approved...")*

There is great value in an intellectual study of Scripture and in the correct understanding of a systematic theology. We *should* strive to wrap our intellects around terms such as *propitiation* as they are used in Scripture and as they enhance our understanding. An intellectual understanding of context points such as cultural idioms and customs will also greatly enrich our correct perceptions of the truths of Scripture, as will a careful study of what the words themselves truly mean in the original language in which they were penned.

My apologies to the *King James Only* crowd, but all translations are *translations*...and none capture all of the shades of meaning originally penned to exact detail in every case. In many cases, an original word cannot be directly translated, as it conveys a spectrum of meanings or concepts, or is veiled by cultural symbolism not understood by the reader. In other cases, words have a much more specific meaning in the original language than was translated into the English. Ancient Greek had six distinct words for "love"... all with varied meanings. Yet all which are used in the New Testament writings were translated to the one English word, "love". Sometimes, a modifier was added to clarify the meaning, such as *brotherly love*; in other usages, we are left to infer the shade of meaning from the context. Therefore, especially when you have uncertainty about a portion of Scripture, examining it in the light of its original culture and language may just provide the fuller understanding you are missing. All of these kinds of intellectual pursuits would be considered part of the *Greek* or *western* mindset approach to Scripture.

The Hebraic Mindset

While the Greek mindset is linear in nature, the Hebraic mindset is much more multi-faceted...and yes, there *is* a reason I chose that specific term. One who employs the Hebraic mindset is like a gemologist who examines the object of study in great depth and detail, from many angles and under a variety of lighting. They seek to more than simply definitively identify what species of gemstone is before them; they pursue a deep and intimate knowledge of this specific stone. They seek fuller understanding of all of its unique characteristics. Beyond chemical composition, physical dimensions, and weight, they analyze its color, clarity, refractivity, trace elements, inclusions, and other aspects of internal structure. They do so under a variety of magnifications and frequencies of light, even utilizing a variety of electronic sensing equipment in these modern times. They put so much effort into becoming truly intimately familiar with each stone because they recognize each stone's potential value, which may be either maximized or destroyed based upon their efforts.

This then is one aspect of the Hebraic mindset in relation to Scripture — the willingness to study it from a variety of viewpoints. Yes, Scripture has very clear, definitive meaning, easily discernable to any who wishes to hear. However, there are also deeper truths and amazing details hidden beneath the surface text. Many fundamental truths of Scripture are only truly grasped by a fuller understanding of all of Scripture — not just a single passage or even a complete book taken on its own. Indeed, many profoundly entrenched misunderstandings of Scripture would be corrected if we took seriously the principle of context, an important aspect of which is placing value on understanding the whole word of God and not just our favorite "pet verses". To the careful reader, Scripture presents important balancing points — a different facet of the same truth — to principles and concepts which are commonly misunderstood.

This is especially prevalent in the Hebrew Scriptures. Consider this poignant passage from

Proverbs 26:4... *"Do not answer a fool according to his folly, lest you also be like him."* Sounds pretty clear, eh? Don't argue with a foolish person. But, wait... read just one verse further... *"Answer a fool according to his folly, lest he be wise in his own eyes."* Proverbs 26:5

----- huh? -----

No, contrary to the conclusion one might jump to here, this is not a "contradiction" in Scripture. It is common in ancient eastern writing, particularly in books of wisdom or philosophy, to present both sides of the story. This is not a contradiction; it is simply presenting a fuller viewpoint, another angle on the same problem. This is known as *reflexive writing*, and much of the book of Proverbs is structured in this manner.

Another aspect of the Hebraic mindset somewhat related to this is the practice of answering a question with a question. Read through some of the accounts of Jesus verbally sparring with the religious leaders — see Matthew 15:1-20 for instance. Take note of how many times Jesus replies to a question with a question of His own.

This is actually a common, even expected rabbinic practice. You see, in the western mindset, the correct answer to, "What is 2 times 3?" is, of course, "6!" But to someone immersed in Hebrew culture, particularly an aspiring rabbi, the correct 'answer' would be something more like, "What is 4 plus 2?" or perhaps, "What is half of 12?" This is answering with the same truth, but from another perspective. It demonstrates a richer, more real understanding of the underlying truth than simply rattling off a memorized, automated answer. After all, even horses or parrots can be trained to answer a math problem correctly, with the proper prompting... and if you ask a dog what's on top of a house, you can get him to say, "ROOF!"

In contrast to the linear thought processes of the Greek mindset, the Hebraic approach may also be seen as more rich in right-brained activity — the seat of emotional response, creativity, and intuition. Here resides the strength of abstract thought and of assembling varied snapshots of truth together into a grander, fuller picture. Here is the ability to perceive connections between things which may at first seem unrelated...to perceive an underlying order beneath apparent chaos. While the left brain is the home of algebra and trigonometry, the right brain handles art, music, and jigsaw puzzles.

When you develop a broader understanding of Scripture and begin also to know God through personal experience, you begin to develop an intuition which both acts more quickly and perceives more deeply than an intellectual analysis of a given situation. You begin to develop more certainty in hearing God's voice and knowing His leading in your life as you begin to catch a glimpse of God's true heart.   We are told that God *"...made known His **ways** to Moses, His **acts** to the children of Israel."* Psalm 103:7

The general population of Israel saw God's actions...what He did. That's great... However, Moses received the better portion. Because he sought to truly know God through relationship — through heart knowledge — Moses came to understand not just the what, but the why. Moses saw God's heart...and grew into a very special knowledge of God and His ways that no other in this band of ex-slaves ever touched upon.

Before I leave this section, please allow me to reinforce a central truth which you may at this point believe me ignorant of: Knowing God is NOT all in your head! In discussing right-brained vs. left-brained, Greek vs. Hebraic thought processes and the like, I have thus far focused primarily on the application of such things to the study of Scripture. Understanding Scripture, of course, is of vital importance in knowing God and avoiding deception. That knowledge of God, however, is not all in your head. God does speak to and through our spirits. I have focused in this section primarily upon the functioning of our minds in knowing God...but the role of spirit shall not be neglected in this complete work. Indeed, it shall be addressed in some detail within the context of discussing the doctrine of the trinity. For now, simply understand this: When God speaks to our spirit, that revelation is brought to our conscious awareness through the integrated functioning of our minds.

Sometimes the revealed word of the Lord to us is a clearer intellectual understanding of Scripture as it applies to our present situation. Sometimes it is a profound revelation of His heart or will in a given difficulty which cannot be attributed to — and often even appears contrary to — an intellectual assessment of that situation. Sometimes, we may receive an "out of the blue" sense of direction or of warning... In any of these cases, the revelation first spoken to and through our spirit becomes known to us through our minds. It is in our minds that we process these revelations and perceptions, and here that we exercise our wills to accept or reject — act upon or deny. God's written word has much to say on the topic of right thinking, controlling what our minds dwell upon, and glorifying God with our minds, whether they be more Greek or Hebraic in nature.

Selah...

This book has been brewing in me for some time. As a writer, when I am being prepared for a new work, I often feel very much like Jeremiah— _"...but His word was in my heart like a burning fire, shut up in my bones; I was weary of holding it back, and I could not."_ Jeremiah 20:9 When I have the time and space to begin the actual writing...well...it generally comes spilling out with abandon! Bearing this in mind, and particularly considering the topic and structure of this book, allow me to ask this of you...read it slowly. There is a Hebrew word which appears 71 times in the Psalms and 3 times in the book of Habakkuk; that word is _selah_.

Not surprisingly, considering its frequency in the book of Psalms, selah is a technical musical term. It is an instruction to pause— a "full rest", if you will. Its purpose is to bring emphasis both to what has just been played (or sang) and to what follows. Strictly translated, it means something like, "Give place to consider..." It serves very much the same purpose in a literary work. This book has an overall "Greek" structure; I am writing from a prepared outline and in a manner consistent with achieving a prescribed overall flow. However, much of the specific content of this book within that framework is rather Hebraic in nature. I will address many topics in the form of individual vignettes...small portions or snapshots of things God has shown me over the years. Because I am a poet by nature, some of the writing will appear in this manner. In fact, I intend to include one entire section of this particular form of expression, as God has frequently spoken deeply profound revelations to me in this way.

For some of you, certain aspects of what I share later in this book may catch you like a right-cross. You may initially be confused, offended, or both. You may be tempted to label me a heretic and hold a book burning. Well, before you reach for those matches, allow me to ask this of you…Selah.

You may find yourself in full agreement with me in some things, thinking, *I already knew that…* You may find yourself leveled by some new understanding of God you had not grasped before… *Oh! THAT'S what that means…* Or, you may simply find certain things that you had believed being challenged — at least from the angle that you had believed them — and determine to pursue a deeper conviction on the truth of the matter from all angles. Nothing could make me happier!

In any eventuality, I encourage you to read one small section of this book at a time. Dwell upon and weigh what is being said. Study the Scriptures in full context for yourself. Take time to simply soak in

God's presence and learn to listen for that still, small voice of revelation. As a married man I can testify to this; many times when we have a hot disagreement with someone, we are both actually saying THE SAME THING —just from a different point of view and in words that the other does not realize are communicating the same central truth.

I do not claim to be a Hebrew or Greek scholar. I hold no theological or other degrees. I absolutely *do not* claim to know or understand everything about God; we will discuss later why this is an impossibility of the absurdist degree. However, one does not require an advanced formal degree to know the one true God who longs for the fellowship of His children. All that is required is a willing heart and the time invested to soak in His presence. I encourage you then, take this time… Read each portion of this book slowly, weighing and considering the contents therein and how it relates to what you already know of God.

You will note, I am sure, the absence of a formal bibliography or abundance of citations. Frankly, the attempt to include such would probably swell this work to the dimensions of a New York City telephone directory and be of little real value. I will occasionally note certain sources, but in this digital age of easy internet access, I trust that you can (and should) explore these topics more on your own. I am of the opinion that we have too much spoon-fed Christianity in this age anyway, and it will do one good to put the effort into hunting down the meat of the Word for yourself. (see Hebrews 5:12-14)

So…Selah! Begin now by turning back to the poem *Ancient of Days* at the beginning of this book. Read each line, each section slowly…dwelling upon what is being said. SEE what is being said. Both writing and reading inspired poetry are good practice for learning to hear the voice of God, as it is an exercise of the intuitive nature.

We will continue next by examining in depth the predicament of sin and death. You may want to brace yourself… It's bound to be a heavy topic.

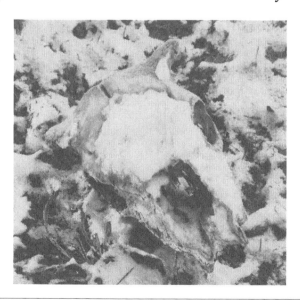

Sin, Death, and Hell

In this section we will deal with what is unquestionably a heavy topic, worthy of sober consideration. I would especially encourage your diligent attention to these matters if you grew up in the church; be certain that you have honestly weighed these matters for yourself and are not merely "riding your parents' coat-tails..." It is most certainly true that God has no grandchildren. If you are not certain, make certain that you have made faith your own.

If you are one who is reading this not yet having made a decision to trust Christ, I dearly hope that this section of this book helps to define for you just WHY it is that we need Him. Christians are often guilty of throwing around theological terms and assuming that an unchurched person will understand what is being said. It is my desire in this section to state as clearly as possible the predicament that Jesus came to save us from. The truth of the concept is so frequently missed because it is, in reality, so simple. Simple, and yet so profound...

Though certainly containing some very serious emotionally charged implications, our examination of these topics will lean heavily upon an intellectual understanding. Sometimes, in our desire to win others to Christ, we rely too heavily upon an emotional appeal. Certainly, appealing to the conscience is a vital aspect in pointing one to their need for Christ, but that is only the doorway. For any decision to truly stick, it needs also to be founded on a rational consideration. We need to understand WHY we believe what we believe. Decisions which are made solely from the heat of emotion are more often than not repented of later... God is not a used car salesman; He presents the whole, sincere truth for you and desires a sincere response...both heartfelt *and* reasoned. Be assured that as you weigh the very serious matters which follow that this is a good news / bad news presentation — you are simply being shown the bad news part first. Stick it out through anything which may bring discomfort...hope is on the way.

We will begin by defining our terms. As we progress, it will become apparent how each of these terms are strongly related, even analogous to one another. They share many of the same definition points, being so identified with one another as to seem to present different aspects of a single state of being — a single essence. Perhaps, just perhaps, a new light of understanding will dawn upon you as we seek to more profoundly grasp the sum and substance of this *unholy trinity*...the root of all sorrow and loss.

Sin

When you hear the word sin, what picture immediately comes to mind? Does a cold shock of fear or guilt strike your heart? Does a dagger of accusation once again plant itself firmly in the forefront of your conscience? Are you thinking now of *sin*, or of *sins*? Our first venture into understanding this topic is in noting the distinction herein. To do so, let us take a closer look at a cornerstone Scripture of evangelism, Romans 3:23.

"for all have sinned and fall short of the glory of God,"

Let us look at that a little more closely than you may have before. There is more here than is often perceived through a casual reading. *"... all have sinned"*... That is written in *past-tense*, and speaks of *actions*...everyone has done wrong things. In case you have never noted it before, what closely follows is a good explanation of the "why" to this "what".... *"and fall short of the glory of God..."* This speaks more of a fallen *condition* or *state of being* leading to those just mentioned fallen actions. This part is also written in *present tense*. We are all born with this fallen sin-nature. Do you doubt me? Try telling a two year old they can't have a cookie... So you see, *sins* are individual wrongful actions, whereas *sin* is the inborn inclination and self-will which leads to these wrongful actions. This is the true heart of the issue.

When we repent and become a child of God through faith in Jesus, we are immediately given a fresh start, a clean slate. All of our sins are forgiven—Jesus already having born the penalty of each and every one. We are also for the first time bestowed with the theoretical possibility of living free of the *condition* of sin, the sinful self-nature. However, anyone who makes the assumption that they will in reality live out the rest of their days without blowing it will find themselves sadly and profoundly disillusioned.

Forgiveness of our sins has already been accomplished; it is a done-deal. However, overcoming the inborn nature of sin is a life long battle which never completely ceases until we reach the grave. We can do nothing of ourselves to earn forgiveness of sins, but we are called to partner with God in retraining our nature to line up with the new life we have been given. We do have a part to play in how we GROW in God… Consider these words from Philippians 2:12-13. *"Therefore, my beloved, as you have always obeyed, not as in my presence only, but now much more in my absence, work out your own salvation with fear and trembling; for it is God who works in you to both will and to do for His good pleasure."*

If grace is a free gift, what exactly does it mean to "work out your salvation"? Do we actually have to do something aside from repentance to earn forgiveness for our sins? Absolutely not! What then is this saying? Turn in your Bible to one closely related parallel scripture — another facet of this particular gemstone — and spend some time in careful contemplation. Sink your theological teeth into James 2:14-16. Take time to get the full picture.

These two Scriptures, along with innumerable others, define the lifelong battle we continue to face following salvation — the daily struggle against the fallen self-nature. Working out our salvation or doing good works is simply on the job training for our new life in Christ. We learn, over time, to live out our new life in Him through individual acts of obedience…becoming renewed and conformed to His likeness. God loves and accepts us right where we are, even if that is face down in a gutter…but He loves us too much to leave us there. We must learn to become new creations in Him.

I like to summarize these just mentioned Scriptures in this way: Information + Application = Revelation. You SEE truth, you ACT on truth, and that truth BECOMES a part of you. This is what Christian growth is all about…living out the truth you know.

Unfortunately, that process of growth never comes easily. The enemy of our souls is always lurking about, scheming. The devil conspires together with the current world system and even our own flesh to entangle us once again in the bitterly seductive threads of the fallen nature. Read again Paul's earlier lament in Romans chapter 7 for a poignant overview of this sad predicament.

The Snare and the Sting of Sin

Galatians 5:16-26 is a vitally important Scripture in understanding this battle between our old and new natures. Indeed, the solution to this predicament is quite succinctly and elegantly stated in verse 16: *"I say then: Walk in the Spirit, and you shall not fulfill the lust of the flesh."* This is indeed a very good summary of the victorious strategy. Let us move on now to put some handles on it.

To truly have a grasp on overcoming our sin nature, we shall endeavor to more fully understand that nature. If we begin to recognize both the snare and the sting of sin from a distance, we shall be much farther ahead on the road to victory. As the ancient Chinese author Sun Tzu penned in The Art of War, "If you know your enemy and know yourself, you need not fear the result of a hundred battles."

The snare of sin and its true nature can be summed up in one word: SELF. All of creation was crafted for one purpose, relationship. God's essential nature is love...giving...to be other-focused. The sin nature stands in direct contrast to this. It is self-focused... selfish. Love focuses on others; sin focuses on self. This may even manifest itself in good works when they are done from a wrong heart...doing good for the sake of feeling good about yourself or looking good to others. This is the chief manifestation of the "I" disease, as I have written of in earlier books.

This desire to focus on self is the very snare of sin. Like any trap, this one is always baited. Read the following passages: Genesis 3:6, Hebrews 11:25, James 1:14. Note the phrases, "good for food", "pleasant to the eyes", "passing pleasures of sin", "enticed and led astray"... Yes, traps are always baited.

Whatever game a trapper is after, he knows where the likely locations are to place the traps, how to hide them, and what to use for bait—what will appeal to the interests and appetites of the intended quarry. Consider for a moment—in what settings or situations do you find yourself most vulnerable? Is it under stress or difficulty, or close on the heels of some level of success? I find that I often lean towards the latter; the enemy does not like victories to stick.

Consider also what bait you seem to most often fall for. Is it pride, self-righteousness, or physical gratification of some sort? The enemy has studied you intently and knows your appetites. God created all things good, but it is the devil's special skill to deceive you into using one of those good creations in a reckless, selfish manner to bring harm and pain upon yourself and others. A hammer can be a wonderfully useful tool, or a dreadful weapon. It all depends on the manner in which it is used.

When we are careless and fall into the trap of self-focus, the trap is sprung. The *sting* of sin is this: loss of relationship…isolation. Our sin does not change the unchangeable God, but it does hide Him from our view. Sin changes us and our perceptions. It is like a dark cloud coming between you and the Sun. The Sun is unchanged, undiminished…but your view is obscured, darkened, confused… (See Isaiah 59:1-2)

So then, to walk in the Spirit is to learn to heed His voice within you, warning you of the enemy's schemes. You may not have even the faintest awareness of a particular trap the enemy has laid in your path, but the God who sees all has perfect knowledge of all of the enemy's devices. Fellowship with the Creator who loves you is the key to avoiding the snares of the enemy. Learn to listen to the right voice within you, and to actively oppose those you know are wrong. Learn and live out the life-giving, relationship focused principles of God's word, not as a duty or out of fear of punishment, but as a love response to the grace He has given. To walk in the Spirit is to commune with the one true God. It is relationship. The choice to *violate* that relationship is the snare and the sting of sin.

Death

"For the wages of sin is death..." Romans 6:23 Death then can very simply be seen as the **state of separation** resulting from one's choice to become focused on self — the choice to separate oneself from the fundamental principle of relationship. Death is the natural result of that choice. It is not so much something which is imposed upon us, but rather the actual choice **we make**. Death **is** separation. The shame, guilt, and other negative emotions resulting from sin further feeds the fires of self-focus which began the whole sad affair. Death feeds death.

We may speak metaphorically about the death of a friendship or of a career. If we adhere strictly to the definition we have detailed above, a literal interpretation in these cases is fully justified. You are **separated from** a friendship or a career. We focus here, however, on physical death and more seriously upon what the Scripture calls "the second death."

The very day Adam and Eve sinned, the direct, face to face relationship they had enjoyed with God died…they found themselves hiding from His presence. They found themselves separate from…and then were even separated from the beautiful Garden and perfect creation the Lord had provided. Their relationship with each other was also gravely damaged…its perfect innocent state tasting of death. More to the immediate point, the *process* of **physical death** was initiated.

The separation they had chosen meant a loss of access to the Tree of Life. As a result of this and of the now fallen state of creation, their physical bodies would be subject to the laws of entropy…would one day wear out and cease to function. If you separate a lamp from its source of power, it goes out. If you separate yourself from the source of life, you die.

Once again, this is not so much a penalty which is imposed upon you, but the actual choice that you have made. You have chosen separation, and God will not violate your free will. This is the natural consequence of physical death — separation of the soul and spirit from the physical body as it ceases to function.

Please be aware — perhaps even warned — that the consciousness does not cease when the body ceases to function. Physical death is not an end to consciousness; it is only a separation from one's physical self and the physical creation. We are created in the image and likeness of God. As such, there is a part of us which cannot cease to be. For some, that is very good news. For others, those who choose continued open rebellion to their Creator, it should be a thing of terror. Remember, death does not mean an end of consciousness, only a separation—a removal to somewhere—just as Adam and Eve were removed from the Garden. We will explore this in greater detail as we next examine the topic of Hell, the ultimate final separation.

Hell

"Hell" is actually an old-English word simply meaning *a hole in the ground*. It was commonly used to reference a root cellar where one would store their carrots, onions, or potatoes for the winter. (No, this is not the origin of baked potatoes…) This term also aptly describes the destination of the physical body upon death—for most of us, a hole in the ground. The essential nature is the same.

Both Hebrew and Greek have specific words for this destination of the physical body upon death, correctly translated in Scripture as "the grave" or similar terminology. You see here that when the body ceases to function, it is removed to a new location…a place of separation. The spirit, having been separated from the physical body, also faces a relocation.

As with the grave for the physical body, both Hebrew and Greek have specific terms for the destination of the spirit upon death. The most common Greek term is **Hades,** the Hebrew, **Sheol.** Turn to Luke 16:19-31 for an apt portrayal of this location. (The account of the rich man and Lazarus the beggar…) You will note here that two locations are actually mentioned; or rather, one location divided into two chambers. One, the location in this parable of the Old Testament saints and righteous dead, was known as "Paradise" or "Abraham's bosom…" Though not yet the experience of Heaven in all of its fullness, it was definitely preferable to the other destination, known as "torments". This second chamber of the departed dead was separate from <u>all</u> of the goodness and blessing of God.

Both of these chambers could be seen as places of waiting. Abraham's bosom was reserved for those who, though imperfect, had desired to know and follow God in their earthly lives. Although not one had a spotless track record, they all aspired to keep covenant with God and desired in their hearts to pursue Him…to know Him…to love Him. In their earthly life, and now in this place of waiting, each of them looked forward in faith to the coming of the Messiah who would redeem them, allowing them to finally enter into the presence of God. This glorious day of liberation was foretold in Psalm 68:18 and fulfilled by Jesus, as we see in Ephesians 4:8-10 and Matthew 27:51-53. Along with Jesus, they became the "First Fruits" of resurrection from the dead, and an end to separation from the Creator.

On the other side of that *great gulf* which separated those two chambers was a place of torments. This is the destination of the rich man in our story. He had lived life...for SELF. He wanted nothing to do with God or His goodness. He chose separation and now, to his sudden, irreversible terror, he found himself the recipient of that wish fulfilled. Up until the moment of his physical death, he had a choice. Now, all choice was gone. He wanted to be separate from, and now he would be...forever.

However, this present destination, Sheol or Hades, is not in reality the rich man's final stop. Remember, this is also a place of waiting. This chamber of 'hell' is something like a county lock-up or prison intake center. Souls here have found themselves arrested by physical death, but have not yet faced their formal trial or final sentencing. That horrifying event is yet future, even from our present time. The final, formal sentencing will simply be God granting lost souls

what they have insisted upon all of their lives —
separation. They have fought against having
anything to do with God. They have desired to be
separate-from. Now that it is too late to change
course, they will unfortunately begin to experience
what that truly means. God is the source of
everything good…all joy, peace, fulfillment… If you
choose separation from the source of every good
thing, pray tell, what is there left to you but torment
and regret?

The name of this final destination of the damned —
the place of ultimate and irreversible separation — is
Gehenna. Two brief mentions of and warnings about
this place can be found in Mark 9:42-48 and Luke
12:5. The time and scene of this final sentencing can
be seen in Revelation 20:10-15 as well as being
foretold by Jesus in the parable of the sheep and the
goats in Matthew chapter 25.

The name *Gehenna* is taken from the valley of
Hinnom, outside of Jerusalem. In ancient Israel, this
was the site of a perpetually burning garbage pit.
Along with general refuse, the bodies of executed
criminals were brought here for disposal by the
occupying Roman forces. In earlier history,
idolatrous kings of Israel practiced child sacrifice at
this location. Its reputation as a place of great evil is
well earned. It is clear to see why the Valley of

Hinnom became a cultural metaphor for the ultimate destination of lost souls.

Throughout Scripture many literal descriptions of the nature of this terrifying final destination may be found. Some of these descriptions include *a lake of fire, a place of outer darkness, possessing an impassible barrier, a bottomless pit, forever, timeless, no escape...* Stretch your mind a moment and consider — these pictures and descriptions are a nearly perfect match for what modern physicists tell us about the nature and characteristics of a black hole!

A lake of fire inside, but dark on the outside (Tremendous consuming energy, but not even light can escape gravity's pull)...

A great gulf fixed at the boundary (the event horizon)...

A bottomless pit (space has collapsed upon itself)...

Forever...timeless... (time slows to a crawl, even stops...the laws of physics break down...and there is no escape)...

Whether or not the Scripture is literally describing a black hole thousands of years before we discovered their existence, this is indeed a good picture of the

ULTIMATE separation, the self-chosen removal from God's creation. This is the fate which awaits all who choose separation and SELF over the glorious relationship for which we were created. This is the second death. Read through Revelation chapter 20 for a detailed accounting in advance of this most terrifying of final appointments. Dwell soberly upon this as a certain reality... This day will come to pass; whether or not you are a part of this particular scene is solely a matter of YOUR personal choice. God has done everything possible to save you from it. It is now solely a matter for you to decide.

SUMMARY

"But each one is tempted when he is drawn away by his own desires and enticed. Then, when desire has conceived, it gives birth to sin; and sin, when it is full grown, brings forth death." James 1:14-15

Here we see once again a succinct outline of the progressive decline into sin and death...the process of separation from the divine Creator and source of all good things. You see the bait, the sinful action, the springing of the trap, and the downward spiral into further separation. The snare always begins with a lie — perhaps the greatest of all lies — that there is something good which God is trying to keep from us. This is always the devils' chief aim: to get us to doubt God's goodness…to cast a shadow upon His spotless, holy character. This is the lie which spawned the fall in Eden, and the root of every snare since. Read just a little farther in the book of James and you will note that we have been warned of this tactic in advance:

"Do not be deceived, my beloved brethren. Every good gift and every perfect gift is from above, and comes down from the Father of lights, with whom there is no variation or shadow of turning." James 1:16-17

God is the creator of all goodness. He delights to bring joy and fulfillment to His children. It is He Himself who created both the desires within us and the fulfillments to those desires. The enemy's scheme is to make us doubt God's goodness, corrupt those desires, and to use what God created for good to bring harm instead. The devil's candy is always poisoned, and there's always a hook.

Always a Hook
There's always a hook when the dark one offers something to entice; what feeds the hunger, fostered by flesh, caries a pitiful price. There's always a lie to lure you back to that which you forsook; before you bite, you should consider, there's always a hook…always a hook…always a hook…

It is my sincerest hope that this portion of this book has in some way broadened your understanding of sin and death, and of our need for God's grace. The really, *really* good news is that, contrary to the lying whispers which may inhabit the darker corners of your heart, God's greatest desire is to rescue you from this predicament. He does not condemn you; He does not simply tolerate you; He loves you with a passion and a reckless abandon beyond mortal understanding. However, He will not force His goodness upon you. You must choose it.

In the next section, we will briefly explore this glorious alternative. We will then more deeply examine what this word GRACE truly means, and finally continue on to learn some more specifics about this one true God, the creator of all goodness. Stay tuned for some very eye-opening, tangible proofs that He can, indeed, be trusted.

Lamentation

We had life…
life simple and complete,
filled with joy and peace
in their fullest measure.
No asphalt…
but stone
and living waters
and flowered meadows.
No smog…
but silver mists
and glassy seas
and unyielding tranquility.

But we chose a lie, thinking God selfish.

And so all of our brittle days
we wander this maddening maze
grasping for Eden.

The Lost

The singer sang a sullen song,
mournful, deep, loud and long.

The dancer danced a dreadful dirge,
maddened by the gruesome gong;

A mournful remembrance
of priceless mercy
that they would not receive,
a pitiful protest
against perfect truth
that they would not believe
forever will echo
in empty places
from those who were deceived.

Secrets

In a time

after time's end,

He ascends above all things

to that realm

where He alone dwells.

He bears a lonely sorrow,

shielded from all other hearts;

a gnawing grief

of shattered hopes

held for those

who would not be reached.

The fullness of all glory

secretly weeps.

The Glorious Alternative

Dreams:

I dreamed a dream of wonderful things, in a land where life was slow; where fountains of grace, freely flowing, refreshed the wandering soul. A gentle path, through valleys bright, along the healing stream, turned back the years to simpler times…when dreamers dared to dream.

What if?

Perhaps the most profound *what if* question one could ever ponder is this: What if Adam had never sinned? What if the fall of man had never occurred? Just what kind of a world would we now — these thousands of years later — inhabit? What would life in 2019 be like if our first parents had listened to and trusted the Father of Life instead of the father of *lies*?

What if questions are rarely helpful when we have blown it in our personal lives. Generally speaking, they tend to be little more than a fruitless distraction which hinders us from moving on and dealing with reality as it now exists. However, in this case we are dealing with a theoretical involving the whole of the human race…*and* with a God who specializes in redemption. His original plan for creation will come to pass; there is no question of that. That glorious alternative is open and available to all who would choose it.

Since the restoration of the Creator's original plan is sure and certain and since this is the topic of our current discussion, there is then perhaps no harm in pondering this particular *what if*. In doing so, I would like to share an excerpt from my previous book, **Grasping for Eden**. Open now the eyes of your heart and indulge in a little sanctified imagination as we reflect upon what might have been...

• •

...As dawn nears, your senses are caressed and aroused by a carefully synchronized unfolding of glory. As you feel yourself waking, you inhale deeply and a warm, gentle breeze perfumed by freshly-flowering honeysuckle greets you. Although the sun is still well below the horizon, it is not dark. In fact, it is never truly dark. The firmament, set in the sky by the Creator, acts as a built-in night light, transferring a portion of the sun's radiance from well beyond the horizon as a gentle pink glow throughout the night.

That same firmament magnifies and intensifies the light of the stars, making them to appear in their true colors. Like molten jewels they shine in myriad hues of yellow, orange, blue, green, red... a cosmic display of grandeur above. Ah, yes! And they *sing* as well! The morning stars quite literally sing for joy! (Job 38:7) Their music travels through the vastness of space as radio waves. The firmament (*Hebrew: "Raqiya"; a thin sheet of metal, most likely hydrogen in its crystalline form...*) tunes in these waves and broadcasts them as audible sound. It fills the atmosphere with a symphony at once soothing and invigorating. Pulsars and quasars keep rhythm and the stars and planets sing together like flutes, oboes, and violins in myriad, ever-changing harmonies, all tuned in the key of C.

You again deeply inhale the perfumed air and open your eyes. You lay in the soft grass of an open field, under a fruit tree on a slight rise. The warm, hairy mass under your head and shoulders shifts slightly and you glance back to see the muzzle of an enormous lion inches from your face. No... there is no fear in your heart, not even the slightest trace. Here, the lion eats grass, not people. (Isaiah 11:7) You recognize this gentle beast as 'Jasper'; the funny little trail of spots on his nose is unmistakable. As his huge, soft, hairy head nuzzles into yours, you reach up and scratch behind his ears, just as he likes it.

You are not homeless; you spend many nights out in this serene meadow not because you must, but simply because you enjoy it. (And, so does Jasper…) A short distance away you have a splendid home, hand-crafted and meeting your every need and desire in every way. But this meadow is one of your favorite places and you never need worry about rain or cold or of falling prey to thieves or dangerous animals. These things simply do not---have not ever existed. Also completely unknown are things like locks, lawyers, doctors, taxes, sleeping pills, politicians, and funeral homes; there's no need for any of those things here. Everyone lives by the law of love and on the very rare occasion there is a misunderstanding or disagreement, chooses to prefer peace to proving oneself right.

You give Jasper one final enthusiastic nuzzle and rise to your feet. You grab a little breakfast from the tree you've slept under and get a long, cold drink from the pure, crystal stream nearby. You stretch the muscles of the perfect body you've lived in for several thousand years now. No gray hairs, or wrinkles, or ulcerative colitis here… You live constantly bathed in the very tangible presence of the giver of life Himself. Never having been separated from that presence by a sinful act of self-will, you know nothing of death or decay. "Good morning, Father!" you whisper to the ever-present glory.

Simultaneously in your spirit and with ears of flesh you hear, *"Good morning. dear child… Won't you come and walk with Me?"*

You spend the next few hours casually strolling and conversing with your Creator. Through meadows and forests and alongside rushing streams you roam, observing the glories of His creation. Plants and animals of every kind and description display the wonders of His wisdom and infinite creativity. Though you have lived thousands of years, each day there are new mysteries and levels of understanding to explore. After all, you are a finite creature, while He is infinite…unbounded in every way. There will never be a time when you run out of things to learn from Him and you cherish every moment you spend with Him on these walks. And He cherishes you.

When the sun has risen high in the sky, you gather with a number of other blessed children of the Creator. There are a few tasks you've decided to accomplish together this day. In another age, or another kind of world, one might refer to this as "work", but here it is a simple joy. There is nothing taxing, stressful, or strenuous in it. It carries a much different purpose here than the unthinkable rationale of *earning one's bread*. Work, here in this world, is simply a means of fellowship, a way to spend time together in a task which benefits all. It is not about earning anything for yourself, but about giving to others and building relationship.

A delightfully vibrant meal is eaten together, followed by childlike games and song. Discussion goes on until very late in the day as each one in turn shares the various jewels of wisdom and understanding they gained from the Great Father that day. Here, people like Einstein and Nicholas Copernicus are on equal footing with others like plain-old Dave Smith or Lisa Edwards. Every individual is endowed with gifts perfectly suited to bless both them and those around them in special, unique ways. There is no prideful ego and no self-loathing shame. Each individual glories in and freely shares the special and particular gifts and revelations granted them and equally cherishes and appreciates those granted to others. There is not the slightest hint of envy anywhere.

As evening comes, a campfire is kindled. Neither the heat nor light is needed, but there is something cheerful in its glow, something which draws friends together around it and silently speaks of wonders none of them yet know how to express in words. As the stars begin to gleam in their full rainbow-brilliance once again, a final joyous hymn is sung in collective adoration to the giver and sustainer of life. Bidding one another good-night, each one strolls off through the meadow, caressed by the stirring of evening breezes. You begin to pace off towards your home, but notice something off in the distance. There, atop the little rise where you began this day, Jasper is waiting for you…

Yes…truly…what a glorious could-have-been world we missed out on! It is easy when you ponder these things to begin to harbor a certain bitterness towards Adam for not simply trusting God and remaining in obedience. Every sorrow mankind has ever known traces back to that one choice to disobey God. And yet, I am fairly certain that if Adam had not made that fatal error…I would have. Every one of us knows what it is to fall short. You see, we are not yet complete… God, however, had already planned ahead for the catastrophe of sin. He will not only restore creation to the glory of Eden, but to glories far beyond even that, for those who choose to receive it.

The Restoration of All Things

"Repent therefore and be converted, that your sins may be blotted out, so that times of refreshing may come from the presence of the Lord, and that He may send Jesus Christ, who was preached to you before, whom Heaven must receive until the times of restoration of all things, which God has spoken by the mouth of all His holy prophets since the world began." Acts 3:19-21

And here it is — the good news…the *really* good news! Although mankind did indeed fall short of God's glory, the all-loving, all-wise Creator had already pre-ordained the solution to this dilemma. Before He even spoke the first syllables of the great creative declaration, "Let there be…" He had already set in motion a plan to redeem mankind, whom He knew would stray. We will discuss the reality of this foreknowledge later; for now, let us focus on some of the general details of that process of restoring creation to its original design and intent.

Mankind is the very crown and focus of creation. Every star which burns in the highest heavens, every jewel from the deepest bowels of the earth was fashioned with mankind in mind. The reason for such extravagance — love! The Almighty God desired a counterpart, an *other-than* to lavish His love upon!

When He spoke the words, "It is not good that man should be alone..." (Genesis 2:18) He was echoing the very cry of His own heart and deepest desires. The very core of God's nature is love, and love never fails! (I Corinthians 13)

And so, after millennia of allowing man the opportunity to realize the futility of his own efforts, God stepped down into creation...and became a man Himself. The infinite, eternal Creator took on the veil of flesh. The Almighty One embraced human frailty. The Lord of the heavens now walked once more upon the dust of Earth—and to what end? He came as a bridegroom, seeking His bride.

This concept of God as a *bridegroom* or *husband* is replete throughout both the old and new testaments. Scripture employs many metaphors for God and His relationship to mankind, but this one is perhaps the most poignant. The late messianic teacher Zola Levitt taught and wrote extensively on Jesus' role as the bridegroom. He spoke often of the direct correlations to Jewish wedding custom inherent in what Jesus said and did in the final weeks leading up to the crucifixion. His words in John chapter 14, "In My Father's house are many mansions...I go to prepare a place for you...I will come again and receive you to Myself..." is but one brief example.

The rapture of the church, when He arrives suddenly to snatch away His bride at the sound of a shout and the trumpet call of God (I Thessalonians 4:16, Revelation 4 and 5) — this is also directly parallel to and reflected in Jewish wedding custom. You see, traditional Hebrew weddings were done a bit differently than what we practice today. Today, we hold the ceremony on a pre-announced date and time. A formal reception and dinner immediately follows and the couple then leaves on their honeymoon.

In ancient times, after a prolonged period of waiting and preparation, the bridegroom would suddenly show up unannounced (as far as the specific day or hour was concerned) to snatch away his betrothed. As he approached, he was required to shout and blow a trumpet in order to give her just a moment's notice to rise and prepare to leave with him. He would then snatch her away and take her to their first home, the bridal chamber (translated "mansion") at his father's property, where they would hide away together on a seven day honeymoon. At the conclusion of this week of being hidden away at the father's house, they would reemerge together to greet the guests who had arrived throughout that previous week. They would then celebrate together a great wedding banquet.

For those of us still alive when the Lord returns suddenly for *His* bride, this snatching away to the Father's house will be our first true experience of Heaven as the corporate **bride of Christ**. This will also be the next phase of God's plan for a full restoration of all things. While the bride of Christ is hidden away with Him for not seven days but seven years, what is known as the tribulation period will be occurring down here on Earth. While this will be the most terrible time ever seen on this planet, many who did not know the Lord before will be finally saved. They will have the honor of being among the guests at the great wedding banquet when we return with Jesus to establish the Millennial Kingdom age. This commences the next phase in the restoration of all things. (Isaiah 9:7, Daniel 9:26-27, Daniel 12:1-4, Zechariah 6:12-13, Revelation chapters 19 and 20)

This Kingdom age, this one thousand year period of glorious peace and prosperity, will indeed be the finest time Earth has enjoyed since Eden. True justice shall prevail. We will be reunited with loved ones whom death had separated us from and enjoy a depth of fellowship never before experienced. The bounties of creation shall explode as nature is brought back into harmonious perfect balance. Hunger and want shall be unknown.

And yet, all is not perfect—not yet. Those who

entered this kingdom age in mortal bodies (not having been part of the rapture) will still retain the capacity to sin. Revelation 20: 1-3 tells us that Satan the great deceiver will be bound for this time — locked away and unable to work his schemes of deception upon mankind. With the glorious Lord of lords reigning in person upon Earth and with peace, prosperity, and great bounty the common experience, sin will be a profound rarity. However, the capacity — the possibility — will still live on in the hearts of those not yet transformed into the eternal state. It is true, my friend, that God looks deeper than men. He sees beyond mere outward performance to the very thought and intentions of the heart. (See Hebrews 4:12)

At the completion of this thousand years, then, what each man truly harbors in his heart will be made evident. Satan will be released for a short time. Then will be one final separating of the wheat and the tares… (See Matthew 13:24-30 and Revelation 20:7-15) As the father of lies leads one final rebellion, all of mankind who retain hearts blinded by pride and willful ignorance will follow that great deceiver in a futile conflict. It will not last long. Judgement will be swift, certain, and irreversible. Every residue of sin will be forever purged from creation. The grave and even death itself shall be consumed in the lake of fire — the second death.

Thus, with the destruction and final removal of all that is unlike God, we shall enter a new eternal age. There will be a new heaven and a new Earth. The Eternal City, more profoundly beautiful than mortal minds can conceive, will come down to the new Earth, "...*prepared as a bride adorned for her husband.*" (Revelation 21:2) All things will be new — restored to God's original intent. No shadow of the fallen creation shall ever dim our hearts again and we shall enjoy wonders which we cannot presently even imagine possible.

This is the glorious alternative which awaits all who would choose to receive it. But what is required of us in this transaction? How does one choose this path over the other? We are told that the road to destruction is *broad* and *easy*, but that the way that leads to life is *narrow* and *difficult*... (Matthew 7:13-14) If God is truly "...*not willing that any should perish*..." (2 Peter 3:9) why does it seem that the way to life is so difficult? And why **do** so many perish, if God does not want it? If the narrow road is the right one, how do we get there? Would it frighten you if I told you that many who **think** that they are on the narrow road...are truly on that other path instead? These will be our next topics of discussion. We shall then take a deeper look at the One making this offer and at some very tangible, mind-blowing proofs that He can, indeed, be trusted.

Echoes of Tomorrow

There's a new world coming. Beyond the flames of ignorance and greed, beyond the cries of despair and the schemes of hateful men, do you hear it? Can you hear the trumpet's voice and the song of Moses and of the Lamb? Do you hear the joyful shouts of the redeemed… echoes of tomorrow?

Can you hear the approaching hoof-beats, pulsing faster… faster… faster… like the heartbeat of a lovesick God, half mad with passion for His bride?

Can you sense; do you know the fire in His eyes… the fires of passion and rage, ready in an instant to pour out vengeance upon the destroyer of men's souls?

There's a new world coming, and the heavens will soon pass away at the voice of His command.

End Note:

In addition to the teachings by Zola Levitt I referred to earlier, I would profoundly recommend that you read The Divine Romance by Gene Edwards. Outside of the Bible itself, this book has had the most profound affect on my understanding of the true heart of God. An inspiring, deeply worshipful novel, it presents all of time and eternity from God's point of view — as the Bridegroom.

The Price of Admission

In his poem *The Road Not Taken* (published in *Mountain Interval*, 1916) Robert Frost describes coming to a place where two roads diverged in a wooded meadow. There he stood for an extended period, contemplating which path to take. After a protracted consideration, he concludes with: "I took the one less traveled by, And that has made all the difference."

Each of us, whether or not we view it as clearly as Robert Frost through the poetic eye, find ourselves at this same divergence of roads. If we accept the premise that it is indeed the narrow, difficult way which leads to life — the one less traveled by — then it is clear what our choice *should* be. And yet, taking those first feeble steps into the glorious divergence eludes the vast majority of mankind. If the road to life is what God truly desires for everyone, why is it so difficult to begin one's journey upon?

Would it surprise you to find out that there's a toll gate at the head of that road? That other road — the broad, easy one — doesn't seem to have one…not as far ahead as you can see, anyway. True, it is rumored that there is some sort of price to be paid at the end of the broad, easy way, but you figure that's something to be worried about later — when it's too late. But here and now, right up front, there's a toll gate at the very head of the narrow way.

You step forward to examine the price of admission: "Perfect moral behavior in thought, word, and deed. A selfless life, given fully and sacrificially in service to others. Total, complete, unwavering obedience to the law of love…" The list continues on, but by now it is clear that no further details really matter. This is already well out of your price range. There's no way you could scrape together even a small part of that. A mixture of sorrow, anger, and confusion washes over you as you stand there, thinking God unjust. You try to find a way to pick the lock or force the gate open, but it is no use. It does not budge.

As you pace away muttering indignantly, you see another traveler approach the gate. You recognize the man at once; it's that bully from fourth grade who beat you up and stole your lunch money at least twice a week. From there, he progressed to stealing bicycles, and from there, to grand-theft auto. He served time for drunk driving and for killing a man in a bar fight. He's now known as a mid-level drug dealer and runs a small prostitution ring.

An acidic, mocking chuckle rises up within you as you mutter, "Yeah…good luck with that, pal!" An odd sort of a look seems to be growing upon the man's face, however — and as you stand there amazed, he drops his head slightly and the gate swings wide open before him! He enters joyfully and the gate swings securely shut once more. Turning to face you fully now, he recognizes you. A weird sort of light covers him and a childlike peace shines out from his eyes. There is a brief flash of regret as he recalls how he had treated you earlier in life. This quickly fades into a knowing plea of expectancy as he meets your burning gaze. "Friend, read on…there is more to know." He motions to the sign on the gate and bids you to investigate further.

Though still clutching a prideful resentment tight to your chest, you decide to take another look. There, at the bottom of the list of requirements for entry, you read: *"Paid in Full by the Builder"*. You then note a long string of Bible verses. Several among these particularly draw your eye.

Isaiah 53:5 *"But He was wounded for our transgressions, He was bruised for our iniquities; the chastisement for our peace was upon Him, and by His stripes we are healed."*

John 3:16-17 *"For God so loved the world that He gave His only begotten Son, that whoever believes in Him should not perish but have everlasting life. For God did not send His Son into the world to condemn the world, but that the world through Him might be saved."*

2 Corinthians 5:21 *"For He made Him who knew no sin to be sin for us, that we might become the righteousness of God in Him."*

A sliver of understanding is just beginning to dawn within you… You read on.

Psalm 34:18 *"The Lord is near to those who have a broken heart, and saves such as have a contrite spirit."*

Psalm 51:17 *"The sacrifices of God are a broken spirit, a broken and a contrite heart – these, O God, you will not despise."*

Proverbs 28:13 *"He who covers his sins will not prosper, but whoever confesses and forsakes them will have mercy."*

So there it is… It seems as though, as far as your part is concerned, the price of admission is simply the *admission* of your need! And this, my friend, is where so many stumble; they refuse to enter by this narrow gate. They do not want to admit their need. The sin nature is born of selfish pride. It both feeds upon and nourishes that pride. Its chief aim is to enthrone self and to exalt one's self-effort. To openly acknowledge need – that you are not complete in yourself – is quite opposite to this. Far too many walk away from the very gate to eternal life simply because they don't want to cope with the fact that they couldn't earn it.

As we have already discussed thoroughly, sin is centered in self. There is no *self-effort* which can rescue us...from self! If eternal life is to be received, it must be received as a gift. There are at least three easily identifiable reasons why this logically has to be the case:

1. Consider the value of what is being offered: Eternal life in a perfect body with all of the pleasures and joys of creation to explore — with no need or desire ever unmet...forever. Question: If it were possible to pay your way into paradise, what could you ever offer to equal this value? There is no sum imaginable which would not be a joke or an insult. It would be exceedingly more feasible to offer a rusty bottle cap in exchange for the Hope Diamond.

2. Everything that you do have — anything that you could offer — you only have because it was first given to you by God. It's already rightfully His.

3. God's design for eternal life is to enable you to reestablish the life giving relationship with Him. He is the very source. God is light and life; the self-nature is darkness and isolation. Self-effort is rooted in pride and by its very nature leads to separation

and death, not life and joy.

To sum this up, a free gift cannot be bought. The price has already been paid by the one offering. Now let us see if we can further illustrate the point by painting a more contemporary picture.

Imagine for a moment that you are in desperate need of a new car. The one you had has breathed its last. It has fully and irredeemably ceased to function. You invested nearly every penny you had trying to keep it running, but to no avail; it has gone to the great beyond of the local automotive bone yard. What is worse is that you live in a very remote area and have absolutely no way to get to a job to earn money to buy another vehicle. You also have no way to get to a grocery store, or money to spend if you could, and the cupboards are bare. That half-bottle of catsup that's left in the refrigerator isn't going to keep you going for long. As you ration out a teaspoon of *last resort*, there's a knock at your door. Curious as to who could be showing up clear out here, you close the refrigerator and pace over to investigate.

You open the front door to find Bob Johnson standing there with a big smile spread all across his face. Bob owns one of the biggest car lots in the state. He explains that an anonymous benefactor has heard of your predicament and has pre-paid for you to come down and pick out any vehicle you'd like from his car lot. All that you need to do is come along with him and receive this free gift. The donor has even made arrangements to pay for all regular maintenance on whatever vehicle you pick out.

You politely thank Bob for his kind thoughts, but inform him that you don't have the money to pay for a new car… "Um, I understand that, " he replies. "You don't *need* to pay anything! It's all been paid for already. All you need to do is come with me to pick it up."

"No…that's ok. I'll get by on my own," you say as you step back and begin to close the door. *Stupid salesman…* you mutter to yourself.

"But…but… You don't understand…it's already paid for! You don't need…."

A bit of prideful anger now noticeable in your voice, you cut him off with, "I told you I don't need your help!" as the door closes abruptly in Bob's face, leaving him standing there in bewilderment.

Do you see now just how foolish this attitude is? Is it any wonder that Jesus spoke so highly of children? Children know how to receive freely. Children harbor no qualms about receiving a free gift. It is only as we grow older — more jaded and weighed down with guilt and pride — that we lose the ability to receive freely with an open heart. But it is only those who are able to receive freely who are also able to give freely with no strings attached. Those able to receive *by* grace are also able to give *in* grace.

God desires a heart of relationship which gives and receives freely out of love, not a contractual commitment of debt and guilt. Every religion in the world, in one form or another, teaches that you must do right in order to be right — you must do whatever particular good works their religion prescribes in order to be right with whatever particular concept of deity they hold. Every false religion the world can offer, at its core, speaks the same lie spoken in Eden... It is about self-effort, and only leads to further isolation.

Only Christianity has the order correct. The true teaching of the Bible is that you *be* right in order to *do* right. You must come to God just as you are; He has already paid the full price in order to restore this relationship, but you must choose it. Relationship can be no other way. Then, as you remain in Him, you are transformed. He, living in unison with your spirit, works to renew your heart each day. You become right through the restored relationship.

Good works are the result of the restored relationship with God, not the cause. The only good works that make that relationship possible to begin with are the ones He accomplished in giving Himself for you on the cross.

■■

As a final conclusion to the current section of this work, I would like to present another excerpt from an earlier book of mine. Let us turn up the light a little and widen the depth of field as we examine another particular facet of truth regarding the meaning of grace. We will make a deeper investigation into the grace which both saves us and leads us on toward spiritual maturity.

Holiness, Humility, and Perfection

Holiness, humility, and perfection: to most of us these are familiar theological terms, but concepts we understand vaguely at best. We know that we are supposed to desire such things... to strive towards them to the nth degree of personal commitment. Yet we never really expect to have any true success. After all, no one is perfect, right? And anyone who thinks themselves to be humble... surely must be mistaken, for that very supposition necessarily disqualifies itself. Somewhere deep inside there abides the accusation that God must simply be asking too much of us. ---And yet, a proper understanding of these terms and how they are applied in Scripture may just birth a new light of hope. Let us briefly examine each of these concepts in turn.

Holiness

In 1Peter1:16, the apostle quotes God Himself from the book of Leviticus: ***"Be holy, for I am holy..."*** This verse, examined solely in its isolated context, would seem to lend credence to the "God expects too much" hypothesis. Before we pass judgment on the Almighty's rationality, however, let us examine the Word a little more closely. If you begin at verse 13 where this train of thought commences, you will gain a clearer picture of what is being said here.

"Therefore, gird up the loins of your mind, be sober, and rest your hope fully upon the grace that is to be brought to you at the revelation of Jesus Christ;" Peter begins by admonishing us to not **freak out**, but to be sober and rest our hope fully on God's grace. It is not by our own holiness that we are to live, but by the grace afforded by Christ's. Peter reinforces this theme in his next epistle, when he marvels at the greatest mystery of grace ever conceived--- the fact that mere flesh and blood *"...may be partakers of the divine nature..."* 2Peter1:2-4

You see, the origin of true holiness is simply realizing how much you lack. "I can't do it...!" That is the genesis of holiness. Holiness is not --can never be and was never intended to be— a product of our grit, determination, and effort. Holiness means coming into a proper understanding of our utter and unqualified need of the One who created us. No amount of human effort can affect true holiness; if we are to possess holiness, we have to *receive* it. There is no other way.

Humility

This, then, leads us to the front door of humility. Humility is a concept truly understood by very few. It may be properly expressed as meekness, but please do not confuse *meekness* with *weakness*. Numbers 12:3 tells us that Moses was the most humble and meek man on the earth in his time, and yet he stood toe to toe with Pharaoh ---the most powerful and ruthless of men. How then could Moses be described as humble...meek?

The best definition I have found for humility is 'to have an accurate picture'. This, Moses had. He knew who and what he was. He was well aware ---perhaps too aware--- of his own faults and failures and shortcomings. When he was called to be God's messenger to deliver His people from Egypt, Moses had even begged God to pick someone else. He knew that he in himself was nothing. Over the next several decades, he would come to understand perhaps more than any other man in history the ALL IN ALL of God. The life of Moses became the simple expression, "I am nothing, He is all."

So properly understood, humility simply means coming into proper relationship to God. He is the creator, we are His creation. He is the initiator, we are the responder. We are His masterpiece, but He is the author and finisher. He is the potter, the poet, the master designer; our hope of glory lies simply and solely in submitting and yielding to the master's work in and through us.

Perfection

In the book of Matthew, Jesus was questioned by a rich young ruler, asking what he must do to be saved. As always, Jesus got to the true heart of the matter. *"If you want to be **perfect,"** Jesus said, "sell what you have and give it to the poor…"* (Matthew 19:21) So… is Jesus implying here that we can buy our way into Heaven? Of course not! Remember, He was directly addressing one particular person, one self-righteous young man, who had directly questioned Him.

In order to understand Jesus' response, you must understand the word he used for 'perfect'. The Greek word *'telios'* is used here. The meaning of this word is "growing towards completeness or in moral character". It does not mean that you have arrived at perfection, but that you are in the process of growth. This young man was failing to make any spiritual progress because his heart was tied to his possessions. Jesus gave him the solution. "Sell what you have... and then come and follow me..."

This same specific Greek word is translated as 'perfect' in Matthew 5:48 and Colossians 1:28. Everywhere it appears, it denotes a process of growth in striving to live a blameless life with the understanding that God alone is *faultless.* It simply expresses an effort, to the best of one's ability, to grow in moral character. It means that you are trying. From the depths of despair and disappointment with myself, I once cried out to God, "How long are you willing to keep forgiving me for this...?" I was honestly surprised to immediately hear, *"As long as you are willing to keep trying!"*

So then, if through God's grace we are striving towards a goal, what is the consummation of that ultimate goal? If our submission to Christ's grace is leading us towards a desired end, what is that end? When will it have arrived, and what does it look like?

There is another Greek term translated as 'perfect', **"teliou-oh".** This means, "*accomplished completeness... no longer in process, but completed and made into a final state of perfection.*" Jesus' high priestly prayer in the Garden of Gethsemane included this term as He poured out His heart to the Father... *"I in them, and you in Me; that they may be **made perfect** in one..."* John 17:23

The author of Hebrews, with one eye in the coming glorious Kingdom age, spoke of being surrounded by a great cloud of heavenly witnesses in the 12th chapter of this epistle. He spoke of both angels and *"the spirits of just men made perfect..."* Men who had been justified by the blood of Christ in their earthly life now... at the consummation of the ages, standing finally complete in the perfection which had always been in God's heart for them.

The apostle Paul reinforces this idea of 'justified now...made complete then' in Philippians 3:12-14. He asserts that he is not yet perfect... not yet complete... but is pressing on towards the mark. He has been justified by the blood of Christ, but was not yet *'teliou-oh'*. Nevertheless, he is committed with his whole heart to be *'telios'*... to keep pressing on.

So, with a proper understanding of holiness, humility, and perfection, you can see that God is no ruthless, unreasonable taskmaster. He will never ask us to make bricks without straw... He knows our frame--- far better than we. He is not difficult to please; all that He desires is a yielded heart to accept

His grace. What does God want from you?

"He has shown you, O man, what is good; and what does the Lord require of you but to do justly, to love mercy, and to walk humbly with your God?" **Micah 6:8**

<u>The Road Not Taken</u>
Robert Frost, 1874 – 1963

Two roads diverged in a yellow wood,
And sorry I could not travel both
And be one traveler, long I stood
And looked down one as far as I could
To where it bent in the undergrowth;

Then took the other, as just as fair,
And having perhaps the better claim,
Because it was grassy and wanted wear;
Though as for that the passing there
Had worn them really about the same.

And both that morning equally lay
In leaves no step had trodden black.
Oh, I kept the first for another day!
Yet knowing how way leads on to way,
I doubted if I should ever come back.

I shall be telling this with a sigh
Somewhere ages and ages hence:
Two roads diverged in a wood, and I—
I took the one less traveled by,
And that has made all the difference.

Comprehending

We have spoken at some length so far as to the great goodness and mercy of God. In the previous section we discussed that there is indeed a price required to satisfy God's justice and to open to us the way to eternal life... However, that price was paid in full by God Himself; this is the "Good News", the very best news of all. This is the news which is quite rightly received with tremendous joy and gratitude by a newly revived soul, alive in the light and glory of freshly received salvation. It is good...to finally be truly alive; the burden of accumulated sins lifted from very weary shoulders.

However, as time passes we begin to feel a new kind of a burden. As we begin to experience the joyous freedom from individual sins of the past, we begin to become aware of something deeper. All is not good — not yet. As Watchman Nee noted in his great work *The Normal Christian Life*, once we have been delivered from the burden of external sins, we eventually discover that something is still very wrong within. We still carry the burden of an indwelling sin nature — a malicious programming which must be fought against daily.

God's re-making of His highest creation begins at the very core of our being; our spirits are revived and brought into unison with Him once more. However, our *minds* are still very much entrenched in this present fallen world. Not only may we find ourselves struggling to overcome already established patterns of sin we've harbored for years, but the world around us — like some sinister computer hacker — assaults us relentlessly every minute of every day, seeking to lead us back into bondage.

Far too often we give in. Forgiveness is still freely available, but the shame of our failure is so much worse now. We **know** truth…we have experienced the goodness of God…we **know** the pain of separation which results from following the bidding of the lower nature…and yet far too often we go for the bait anyway. A prolonged struggle in any area of besetting sin is likely to lead to deeply felt despair. We can come to a place of simply wanting to give up…to stop trying. It is not that we doubt God's mercy; it is simply that our own sense of justice is awakened and we simply do not understand how even God could forgive us for doing that same thing…yet again. The human mind cannot really grasp the concept of *infinite* anything — infinite mercy least of all.

The secret to embracing the full richness of God's goodness and mercy may just lie in coming to a fuller comprehension of His attributes. We must obtain a fuller picture of who He really is. I guarantee you without reserve that every one of us has a far-too-small picture of God. The depth of knowledge held by the most brilliant theologian ever to live does not even hint at scratching the surface. We shall never have full understanding of all there is to know of God. However, He does want us to know Him as we are able and has taken great pains to reveal Himself to us. We can know enough to more fully trust His goodness.

So let us now focus upon a few key attributes of God and ponder a little more deeply the implications of these great truths. Let us examine some of the traits which define the being of God, those things which are the essence of who He is and are only true of Him. In coming to a fuller understanding of who God truly is, we may find ourselves more able to understand and receive His forgiveness — yet again.

God in His Natural State
We shall begin this journey by delving into what is surely the most difficult mental exercise ever conceived of. We will attempt to picture in some small measure God in His natural state — the true fullness of God — God as He was before the first act of creation. Laying hold of a basic understanding here is key to comprehending the other attributes we will discuss. This is the foundation stone for

understanding the absolute, truly unique identity of the creator.

Genesis 1:1 reads, "In the beginning God created the heavens and the earth." Have you ever thought to ponder *where* God was when He created thusly? He could not have been in the universe, as that is what was being created…the universe we know, as well as the heavenly realms, invisible to our eyes. The Bible opens with the creation of both realms invisible to us and with everything which frames our existence — everything which we are equipped to perceive, experience, and interact with. All time, space, matter, and energy have their origin at this one point. But what was before the beginning? Where was God when He spoke all of these marvels into being? Have you ever pictured God…in whatever mental context you would place Him…afloat in some great endless sea of blackness? Did you think that He just suddenly had the thought, *You know, it's kinda' dark here. Maybe I'll create light to spruce things up a bit. Kind of empty too…maybe some stars and planets wouldn't hurt…..then maybe people!*

Here is the first mind-blowing truth about God: Before the creation of the heavens and the earth, He wasn't anywhere! There was no "anywhere" for Him to be. There was not God and empty space; empty space did not yet exist. There was not God *and* anything! There was **only** God...infinite, eternal, without origin or limitation of any description. He was literally the ALL. It is of no use to ask how long ago this was, because time did not yet exist; time is a property of the physical creation. This 'time' was *before* time!

Now, our mortal minds cannot truly grasp this. Everything we know, everything we have ever experienced, had a beginning. Everything we know, even the universe as a whole, has limits and a defined size (even if in a state of expansion). But God in His natural, true state — is above...outside of time and space. He predates the universe and is self-existent, without a starting point. There is no way one could ever see all of God, as you would need to be at some point outside of Him to do so...like looking at a friend across the room. Being truly infinite, there is no place *outside of Him* to be. Outside of Him does not exist. This small fact brings us to the first of three theological terms we will discuss in understanding the attributes of God.

Omnipresent
This term very simply means that God is everywhere at once. He can hear your prayers and be tangibly present with you at the exact same instant that He is tangibly present at a prayer meeting in Shanghai, China. In our mind's eye we may picture

this truth as being explained that God is *very big*. However, we rarely ponder just how big He really is. Think back a moment to what we discussed about God in His natural state. We said that there was no such thing as outside of God. Therefore, it follows that the physical creation — all of it — took place the only place that it could, inside of Him.

Many eastern religions and universalist cults worship things like rocks, trees, monkeys, and rats. They do so in the belief that "God is in all things..." This is a destructive fallacy. They think too small; the real truth is that, in a *geographic* sense, all things are IN GOD. It is true that much evil exists in our world...much that is unlike God. Those elements will ultimately be dealt with and end forever. We speak here solely in terms of location, not comparative morality. Since there was nothing besides God prior to creation, not even empty space, it follows that all of creation — all time, space, matter, and energy — is inside of His being. This is how He can be quite literally everywhere at once.

I have stressed repeatedly up to this point one cannot truly see God, as He is infinite. I am sure that it has crossed a few minds that Moses is said to have seen God on Mount Sinai. (See Exodus 19, 20, 24, 33, 34....) Isaiah and other prophets are also said to have had visions of God...so how can it be said that no one has, or can, see God? Well, recall that I said, "in His fullest sense…" God can and does enfold Himself down into and directly interact with the physical creation. This is exactly what He did when He took on human flesh in the person of Jesus…as we are told in Colossians 2:9, *"For in Him dwells all the fullness of the Godhead bodily;"*

Hebrews 1:3 speaks of Jesus, *"…who being the brightness of His glory and the express image of His person, and upholding all things by the word of His power, when He had by Himself purged our sins, sat down at the right hand of the majesty on high."* I would urge you to read this entire chapter in context to obtain a fuller picture of what is being spoken of Jesus here. However, for the purpose of our current topic of discussion, we will stick to this one verse. The specific terms *brightness* and *express image* provide the answer to our present quandary. The specific Greek term used for **brightness** finds its sole usage in Scripture right here and literally means *out-radiating*. Taken along with **express image**, we can begin to piece together an idea as to how God who is invisible to us because He is infinite can none the less make Himself known—how the invisible God can be visible!

So, what is the solution to this ultimate "can't see the forest for the trees" quandary? The infinite, almighty God can manifest a localized, representative image. Have you ever concentrated the light of the sun through a magnifying glass? If so, you have produced a localized, representative, exact image of the Sun, even carrying with it the power of its source, as it will set alight anything flammable. The image appears directly in front of you, but is still tangibly and continuously connected to its source some ninety-four million miles away. It is at once a few inches from your hand *and* tens of millions of miles away. It is both places at once. In like manner, the infinite God can both dwell in inapproachable light far beyond the fires of the big bang…and stretch out upon a rough and bloodied wooden cross at the same time. So if you've ever wondered if God really sees you in your daily struggles, be most certainly assured that He does. He is literally, tangible present, waiting to render immediate aid if you will but turn to Him.

Omniscient

So if God is truly everywhere at once and can see everything at once, it would logically follow that He is *omniscient*; He is all-knowing. He knows everything about the workings of the physical creation. He knows every detail of everything which has ever happened. He knows every detail of everything which is currently, this moment, happening everywhere. This is a difficult enough concept to grasp, but I would like to throw something even more mind-blowing at you — He knows every detail of everything that ever *will happen* as well!

He knows what the exact price will be for every stock on every world exchange for every second of every day. He knows the exact date, time, and location every human yet to be born will take their first breath…and their last. He knows every detail of every point in the future just as well as He knows every detail of the past and present; they are all the same to Him. Before we discuss the implications of this, let us take a brief glimpse of just a few of the Scriptures which support this premise.

"Remember the former things of old, for I am God, and there is no other; I am God, and there is none like me, declaring the end from the beginning, and from ancient times things that are not yet done, saying, 'My counsel shall stand, and I will do all my pleasure.'" Isaiah 46:9-10

"Known to God from eternity are all His works."
Acts 15:18

Now, one could take these first two examples to be saying that God simply decided to do certain things from the very beginning. This would not necessarily be foresight as we are discussing it. However, the need to do those things, such as the work of the cross, would certainly need to be foreseen. In any event, many more concrete examples exist.

Numerous prophecies throughout the Old Testament foretold exact events in excruciating detail hundreds of years in advance. The great messianic prophecies of Isaiah chapter 53 would be one such example. Genesis chapter 15 would be another. Here God tells Abraham of his descendants' bondage in Egypt and eventual deliverance, including the exact duration of their sojourn in Egypt, and what portion of the total time would be under the yoke of slavery. All of this was spoken to Abraham far in advance of the birth of his first promised child.

Even Jesus' "triumphant entry" into Jerusalem on what is known as Palm Sunday was foretold hundreds of years in advance, including the *exact day* on which it would occur. Jesus rode into Jerusalem on a lowly donkey (in accordance with Zechariah 9:9) 483 years to the exact day from the countdown starting point given in the prophecy of Daniel 9:24-27. As He entered, Jesus wept over the city, foreseeing its destruction in 70 AD; a destruction which would come upon it, "because you did not know the time of your visitation." (Luke 19:42-44)

We see that Jesus foreknew the betrayal and

rejection He would face, even speaking of it at length well in advance with his apostles. He had known from before creation that He would face this trial. He came into the world specifically for this purpose…to bear the sins of all mankind. He was completely aware that He was, "the lamb, slain from the foundation of the world…" (Revelation 13:8) Before He formed Adam from the dust of the ground, He knew — He foresaw the day that He would take upon Himself the form of mortal flesh and shed His own blood to redeem His beloved creation. YOU are a part of that beloved creation.

"Blessed be the God and Father of our Lord Jesus Christ, who has blessed us with every spiritual blessing in the heavenly places in Christ, just as He chose us in Him before the foundation of the world, that we should be holy and without blame before Him in love, having predestined us to adoption as sons by Jesus Christ to Himself, according to the good pleasure of His will, to the praise of the glory of His grace, by which He has made us accepted in the Beloved." Ephesians 1:3-6

One could share many additional Scriptures in support of the foreknowledge of God, but I believe we have established a sufficient foundation. In trying to wrap our minds around this concept, let us take a brief look at an illustration Chuck Missler employed in several of his teachings on this topic.

He referred back to the infinity of God and the fact that all of creation is, geographically speaking, inside of Him. Therefore, God in His natural state is outside of / above the space-time dimension. Chuck Missler likened this to an observer in a helicopter or a blimp hovering far above a holiday parade. The parade route he likened to the passage of time, with the starting point being creation and the end point being the initiation of the eternal ages. Time, like a parade route, is a finite thing.

Now, any participant in the parade knows only where they are presently at, and can perhaps recall the recent past block or so. However, they really have absolutely no certainty of what lies ahead. All they can do is follow the flow — the flow of time — and find out what is next as they come to it. They are stuck in the space-time dimension and can only see the future in that one instant where it becomes their present.

For the observer hovering far above, in another plane of existence, the story is quite different. They can see it all at once. They can see every point along the route…every moment in time…simultaneously. To them — to God — there is no past, present, and future as we know them; there is simply *the eternal now*. Yes, there is a passage of events, the observer on the higher plane can see all events at once, even those which *from our point of view* have not yet occurred.

One final note before I leave this illustration; the observer far above — God — may indeed see everything at once, but that does not mean that He is the cause of everything which happens along the route. If a clarinet player cracks a reed and squeals incessantly, it is not His fault. If someone from the crowd lobs a grapefruit down the bell of one of the tubas, the observer is not to blame. If someone foolishly lined up the horses in the *front* of the lineup…well, you get the picture. Foreknowledge is not the same as causation. Just because you are aware of someone's wrong choices before they make them does not mean that you are responsible for their wrong choices. Each individual bears the privilege and the responsibilities of free will. God will not violate that.

On a personal note, there have been a few occasions where I have experienced first-hand the reality of God's foreknowledge. Without going into excessive detail, God has occasionally shown me brief glimpses of my own future in advance through dreams. These dreams have on one or two occasions contained extraordinarily precise detail — in one case, down to the exact content of a drawer in the lobby of a building I had never been inside of. On this occasion,

God had a very specific reason for blowing my mind in such a manner. He was speaking very clearly to me, "Pay attention! I have something for you here..."

This particular occasion was a Young Life weekend retreat at Camp Field in Camas, Washington. The guest speaker for the weekend was a retired missionary speaking on *why you should go to the mission field...* God had already begun to place this call upon my heart, and I guess really wanted to drive the point home that weekend.

A couple of hours after arriving at a camp I had never been to before but that looked oddly familiar, one particularly powerful visual image triggered the memory of a recurring dream I had been having over the previous year. I very literally went down on my knees in the snow as the extremely detailed *memory* of the weekend I was *about* to live through came flooding into my mind. The songs and skits at chapel time, the evening activities, the insides of all of the buildings, things people would say to me....I had seen them in every detail before. The above picture of the dime I have glued in the songbook I used that weekend, and still have in my possession. I saved it as a little token memento and reminder to me of this occasion. I found that dime underneath one specific stepping stone on a quarter-mile long trail at night in the snow, very shortly after that one image triggered the memory of the dreams. How did I know which one specific stone among hundreds to flip over to find this dime? I had first found that dime in that recurring dream…and now knew which specific stone it was underneath. Yes…God got my attention that weekend in south central Washington, and I am currently in my thirtieth year engaged in full time ministry and missions.

I know with certainty that God knows every detail of the future. For now, **we** are stuck in this sometimes rather unpleasant parade and have to live it out as it comes. We do not have the privilege or ability to see as He sees, but we can learn to listen for correction and direction from above, and learn to trust His guidance; He knows where the horses have been…

It can be very discouraging when we get out of step or our instrument plays out of tune, but there can be comfort in knowing that God sees not only where we are now, but where we are going. He knows that we are in a process of learning and growth. What we are now is not our final state. He loves us where we are now and is committed to sticking with us as we grow and learn to be better. We are His children. He is our perfect, loving father, committed to helping us grow beyond what we are now to what we shall one day be. A more glorious future awaits followers of Christ than we could possibly conceive of from our current vantage point. Hold on to courage. Embrace hope. When you fall, stand up and continue on by His grace.

"Behold what manner of love the Father has bestowed on us, that we should be called children of God! Therefore the world does not know us, because it did not know Him. Beloved, now we are children of God; and it has not yet been revealed what we shall be, but we know that when He is revealed, we shall be like Him, for we shall see Him as He is. And everyone who has this hope in Him purifies himself, just as He is pure." 1John 3:1-3

Omnipotent

This term means *all-powerful*. I do not feel it necessary here to spend a great deal of time fleshing this out. Surely you would acknowledge that the supreme being who simply spoke all of the vastness of the cosmos into existence…could not possibly have any competition in majesty or power. There is simply nothing that He cannot do.

There are, however, things that He *will not* do. He

will not violate free will. He will not violate His word. He will not force His goodness upon anyone — relationship must be a free-will choice. One of the best illustrations of these principles is to be found in the story of the prodigal son (Luke 15:11-32)

Even though the father in the story knew that his younger son was headed for trouble, he would not violate the son's free-will choice. He would not try to force continued relationship upon his child, knowing that would perhaps drive the son farther away emotionally. The father had the wisdom to know that perhaps his child would have to learn some lessons the hard way, and so he allowed him the freedom to do so.

The father did not run after the child when he left, but he did run out to meet him when he had learned his lesson and desired to return home. Mercy is free, but it is never forced. Just as the prodigal son in the story learned, anyone who truly comes to themselves while lost in the mire of sin will find a merciful, gracious father waiting at home, eager to receive you back and restore you to wholeness. The son returned home in humility, hoping perhaps to be taken in as a servant. The father, however, joyously received him back as a son.

The father had certainly held the power to deny his

son's request to receive his inheritance early. He could have exercised the reigns of authority which were rightfully his and forced the son to remain at home. However, in his great wisdom the father knew that there was something amiss in his child's heart which could only be remedied through allowing his child to discover for himself his own foolishness and inadequacies. In great, aching sorrow, he watched his wayward child depart. He relinquished the control he could have exercised to keep his child from leaving, in hopes that the son would one day return from his foolish and selfish wandering. And so is God with us. Whenever we return home in honest brokenness and humility, He joyously waits with open arms. Yes, our God is all-powerful; that power is best and most acutely displayed in the titanic, unfathomable depths of His great mercy. If you have been away in foolish wanderings, do not fear to return home.

"...Mercy triumphs over judgement." James 2:13

And so we conclude our brief overview of some of the attributes of God. Entire libraries could very well be penned on each individual point, but literary overload is not our purpose here. I have simply desired to provide a very brief glimpse — a starting point toward deeper understanding. I have wished to simply awaken within you a renewed appetite to pursue on your own a more intimate knowledge of

God. It is also my hope that you may find the courage to return home from whatever prodigal wanderings you may personally experience. This is our common heritage as members of a fallen race, in the process of redemption. The Father waits with open arms.

"There is therefore now no condemnation to those who are in Christ Jesus, who do not walk according to the flesh, but according to the Spirit. For the law of the Spirit of life in Christ Jesus has made me free from the law of sin and death." Romans 8:1-2

<u>Conclusion</u>

I would like to conclude this book by sharing a brief compilation of some of the deeper things I have discovered over many years of studying God's word. Though the depth of even the plain surface text of Scripture is certainly sufficient to fill one's life to overflowing with treasures of wisdom and grace, an infinite God has penned an infinite book. The original languages of Scripture operate on levels of revelation far beyond the English text…and so much lies beyond the surface. Again, this is just a small, cursory taste. There is much, much more I had planned to share in this book on these particular areas of study, but I feel God laying on the reigns…telling me not to overload the reader with too much that may distract from the overall theme of this book and His purposes for inspiring me to write it. Hence, what I share here is not even scratching the surface of this topic of study, but will perhaps inspire you to investigate more on your own. Entire libraries could and have been written on the following topics and more.

Allow me to be clear up front…knowing these things in no way affects your salvation. No Hebrew or Greek scholar is any more saved than the average seven-year-old believer who knows little more than, "Jesus loves me, this I know…" I simply share this brief glimpse of deeper things to more impress you with the glorious wisdom and goodness of God. I also wish to put within your reach the assurance that the Word of God is truly the holy writ of an infinite being. it is no man-made collection of fables; of that you can be certain. Perhaps a new wonder of and reverence for Scripture will draw you closer to its true Author. This is my desire here. Following this brief treatise, I will wrap up by sharing some more poetry and prose born out of intimate times of fellowship with "Daddy God"… Thank you for sticking with me this far. I pray that you are blessed by the following.

The Living WORD

This is lengthy and a little academically thick, but I believe you will be blessed if you take the time!

I have shared some on this before, but will add a bit to it this time... I have been doing some FASCINATING study on some of the "deeper" things in the Bible, beyond the plain text, at least as it is rendered in English. You see, Hebrew is a pictographic language.... Every LETTER has a conceptual meaning which both helps to define the word it is in and amplify its meaning. Additionally, words are frequently made up of smaller words, which serve the same purpose.

One simple example: "Abba"...which is an informal term for "father" akin to "Daddy". In Hebrew, it is two letters... Aleph and Bet. Aleph stands for the head, chief, the highest position..... Bet, originally a picture of a tent, stands for the home or dwelling place. So, "Abba" / "Father" defines itself as "Head of the house".

Now, let's take a brief look at just a few examples where Jesus is portrayed in the Old Testament... and His identity as the very Creator.... Take a moment and look up Revelation 5:6 and Revelation 13:8. Stick a thumb in Zechariah 12:10----- we'll come back to that later... In Revelation 13:8 we see Jesus identified as "The lamb, slain from the foundation of the world..."

Ask yourself, where does one find "the foundation of the world?" Why, Genesis, of course! How about the very first chapter? The First verse of the first chapter? Why....what about the very first WORD? That's right... the very first WORD of the Bible speaks of Jesus! It speaks of Him that lamb slain....from Revelation. How, you ask? Remember those meanings of letters? (and smaller words)... Let's take a look...

The first 3 words of the Bible, in Hebrew, are "Barasheet bara Elohim..."

The first word, rendering by word portion (bar-a-sheet) reads, "The Son of the Highest will be destroyed by His own hand and effort on a cross"! If you break it down further, to every single letter, it carries the same meaning! "The house of the highest God will be destroyed by His own hand and effort on a cross..." How is this the same? In Jesus, "...all the fullness of the Godhead dwells bodily" (Colossians 2:9) and Jesus referred to Himself as the temple or dwelling place of God.... (John 2:19-21).

Move along to the second word.... John 1:1-3 tells us plainly that Jesus IS the Creator... and that He made everything...and nothing was made apart from Him. The second word of the Bible states this... "BARA" means "created... the act of creation" and broken down into parts, says, "the Son of the Highest"..... ("bar"= son of, a (aleph) = the highest)... So, the "Son of the Highest IS the creator!

Ok, third word... "Elohim"... This is the word translated "God" here.... it is a funny sort of word, meaning a compound singular.... basically one thing composed of more than one part or expression, but in full unity. This points to the doctrine of the trinity.... If you have a problem understanding this, God Himself has given us a picture... MAN, created in God's image and likeness (Genesis 1:26) is also a trinity! Body, mind, and spirit...in full unity, composing ONE BEING! Jesus IS GOD the CREATOR! Remember when He said, "Before Abraham was, I AM"? (John 8:58). He was identifying Himself as the Creator God, using the very Name of God as spoken to Moses... Yahweh... (Exodus 3:14)

Now, "Yahweh" is 4 letters in Hebrew... YOD, HEH, VAV, HEH. What does that "say" by the meanings of the letters? Again, this points to Jesus..... "The hand......Behold in wonder....The NAIL.... Behold in wonder!"

There is something I have recently discovered.... a word (well not exactly... but two letters which carry a meaning) which have NEVER been translated out of the original Hebrew! What would be the 4th "word of the Bible" if it were a word....?

Ok... take a peek at Revelation 21:6. Here we see Jesus portrayed as "The ALPHA and the OMEGA...." The first and last letters of the Greek alphabet, signifying "the beginning and the end"... The Hebrew equivalents to these letters are ALEPH and TAV. This is the two letter combination, appearing in the Original Hebrew, which has never been translated...not into the Greek Septuagint, not into the Latin Vulgate, not into English or any other language... I am sure because the translators didn't know what to do with it! But as you have seen, it carries the same connotation as "The Alpha and Omega" in Greek... So for ease of understanding, we will substitute that more familiar term. So, where does this appear? Oh, yes.... Right after "Elohim" (God) in Genesis 1:1..... connecting Jesus (the Alpha and Omega) in Revelation even more directly to being the incarnation of the very Creator...dwelling in human flesh.

Oh, yes...... it gets better........ Flip over to Zechariah 12:10....   This should be very familiar to you as one of the most famous prophecies of the coming Messiah..... That ALEPH-TAV appears here as well.... Read with it included, by connotation, we see:

"And I will pour out on the house of David and on the inhabitants of Jerusalem the Spirit of grace and supplication; then they will look on Me – Aleph Tav – (THE ALPHA AND THE OMEGA)--- whom they have pierced; they will mourn for Him as one mourns for his only son, and grieve for Him as one grieves for a firstborn."

One final note... the Aleph, as we have seen, carries the meaning of the chief, highest position...God being the ultimate expression of this, of course. TAV was originally a pictograph of a signpost of sorts....something lifted up to be noticed....to be looked to... as in the bronze serpent in the wilderness, foreshadowing Jesus. (Numbers 21:9, John 3:14) In the original paleo Hebrew, it was drawn as two crossed beams—a cross. So, this two-letter untranslated expression, pointing to God in such significant places as discussed here.... Identifying Jesus as the Creator... also, read literally, could be seen to portray God, the Highest, on a cross.... Aleph - Tav........ The Alpha and the Omega, who gave ALL for you.

Now, this ALEPH -TAV concept can be found one other place in Scripture, although it is not directly written in the text. You have to extrapolate a little. As the late Chuck Missler liked to emphasize, every detail of the Bible is there for a reason. In the first two chapters of the book of Numbers, we are given quite a bit of detailed information about the organization of the camp of Israel as they traveled through the wilderness on the exodus from Egypt. God specifically ordered every detail of how they were to travel, and how they were to encamp. When they were to encamp, they were specifically divided into four groupings. Numbers lists these groupings, even going as far as to list the populations of each tribe. Moses and the Levites were to camp in an area occupying the very center, surrounding the Tabernacle. The tribes of Judah, Issachar, and Zebulun were to camp directly east of the tabernacle and the Levites. Reuben, Simeon, and Gad were to camp directly south. Ephraim, Manasseh, and Benjamin were to camp directly to the west...and finally, the tribes of Dan, Asher, and Naphtali were to camp directly to the north.

Now it is time to use a little math. Remember that the population of each tribe is given. Assume an average number of people per tent and draw this out on a piece of graph paper, with a spot in the middle for the Levites and the Tabernacle. The picture which results from this little exercise is fascinating. The camp of Israel would have appeared from above as a giant TAV, a perfect cross, laid out on the desert floor, with the Tabernacle, the tangible presence of God, dwelling at the very center. Remember, the ALEPH means *the highest one...* So here, again, you see the Highest One (God) on a cross... It is no wonder that later in the book of Numbers, when being bribed to curse Israel, the prophet Balaam could not do so. As he looked down upon the encampment of Israel from above, he was seeing the ultimate redemptive plan of God for ALL people laid out before him — literally spelled out on the desert floor some fourteen centuries in advance.

Ancient Semitic/Hebrew							Modern Hebrew			Greek			Latin
Early	Middle	Late	Name	Picture	Meaning	Sound	Letter	Name	Sound	Name	Ancient	Modern	
⊳	✝ ⅄	א	El	Ox head	Strong, Power, Leader	ah, eh	א	Aleph	silent	Alpha	A	A	A
⊔	⅁	⊐	Bet	Tent floorplan	Family, House, In	b, bh(v)	ב	Beyt	b, bh(v)	Beta	B	B	B
✓	⅂	λ	Gam	Foot	Gather, Walk	g	ג	Gimal	g	Gamma	Γ	Γ	C G
▽	△	⅂	Dal	Door	Move, Hang, Entrance	d	ד	Dalet	d	Delta	Δ	Δ	D
ⵌ	⅁	⊓	Hey	Man with arms raised	Look, Reveal, Breath	h, ah	ה	Hey	h	Epsilon	E	E	E
Υ	↗	ך	Waw	Tent peg	Add, Secure, Hook	w, o, u	ו	Vav	v	Digamma	F		F
⅃	⅃	١	Zan	Mattock	Food, Cut, Nourish	z	ז	Zayin	z	Zeta	Z	Z	Z
ⴲ	ⴲ	⊓	Hhet	Tent wall	Wall, Outside, Divide, Half	hh	ח	Chet	hh	Eta	H	H	H
⊗	⊗	ɵ	Tet	Basket	Surround, Contain, Mud	t	ט	Tet	t	Theta	Θ	Θ	
⅃	⅄	ⸯ	Yad	Arm and closed hand	Hand, Work, Throw, Worship	y, ee	י	Yud	y	Iota	I	I	I J
⊎	у	⅃	Kaph	Open palm	Bend, Open, Allow, Tame	k, kh	כ	Kaph	k, kh	Kappa	K	K	K
∠	↙	ⸯ	Lam	Shepherd Staff	Teach, Yoke, Authority, Bind	l	ל	Lamed	l	Lamda	Λ	Λ	L
⌇	⅂	⅂	Mem	Water	Water, Chaos, Mighty, Blood	m	מ	Mem	m	Mu	M	M	M
↘	⅃	⅃	Nun	Seed	Seed, Continue, Heir, Son	n	נ	Nun	n	Nu	N	N	N
⅂	⅂	⅂	Sin	Thorn	Grab, Hate, Protect	s	ס	Samech	s	Xsi	Ξ	Ξ	X
◌	o	у	Ghah	Eye	See, Watch, Know, Shade	Glottal Stop	ע	Ayin	silent	Omicron	O	O	O
⅃	⅃	⅃	Pey	Mouth	Open, Blow, Scatter, Edge	p, ph(f)	פ	Pey	p, ph(f)	Pi	Π	Π	P
⊦	⅄	⅄	Tsad	Trail	Trail, Journey, Chase, Hunt	ts	צ	Tsade	ts	San	M		
ⅅ	⅁	⅄	Quph	Sun on the horizon	Condense, Circle, Time	q	ק	Quph	q	Qoppa	Ϙ		Q
⅀	⅃	⅂	Resh	Head of a man	Head, First, Top, Beginning	r	ר	Resh	r	Rho	P	P	R
⌇	w	⅄	Shin	Two front teeth	Sharp, Press, Eat, Two	sh	ש	Shin Sin	sh, s	Sigma	Σ	Σ	S
✝	✕	⅂	Taw	Crossed sticks	Mark, Sign, Signal, Monument	t	ת	Tav	t	Tau	T	T	T
⅄			Ghah	Rope	Twist, Dark, Wicked	gh							

"Hebraic Letter Meanings" chart courtesy of The Ancient Hebrew Research Center.

Adrift

Like some long-discarded feather tossed by the
breeze, or a cork drifting aimlessly upon an
angry sea, life comes by surprise...

A thousand helpless questions rise from a
desperate heart, but the sky above seems brass
and answers are denied.

These are the times we learn
to know what we really know;
it is the breath of God
which carries us on---
and in these storms we grow.

Father of life,
shine down on me;
renew my soul
and set my heart free
to fly on the wind
and dance on the sea.

A Gift of Dandelions

A gift of dandelions, given by tiny hands, smiling eyes of wonder, blazing with starfire… eyes perfectly trained to see Heaven's majesty in the smallest things of earth. "For YOU, Daddy!" Three tiny words present a priceless gift…something so common, yet given with love of uncommon measure, uncommon depth, uncommon trust, and absolute abandonment to joy.

Tiny hands, so like mine, though as yet unstained by sin… With trembling eagerness and rigid commitment, they reach up, bearing a worthless gift, made precious beyond measure by the love with which it is offered.

In blatant simplicity, all the wisdom of the ages is spoken, and all the stupefying wonders of creation, made plain, and all the purpose of being… revealed.

For the hands that fashioned all things fashioned all things for this purpose: the love which bestows immeasurable value upon even the common… love which sees through eyes unglazed into the heart of another.

The hands which fashioned all things delights to receive whatever is given from a pure heart, be it gold or dandelions… for the heart which gives far outweighs the gift.

Tiny hands, washed by divine blood: with trembling eagerness and rigid commitment, I reach up, bearing a priceless gift of self… my dandelions. Gazing through aqua skies with eyes renewed by wonder, I whisper, "For YOU, Daddy!"

A Present Help

Do not fear the future,
nor be enslaved to past regrets,
nor doubt the grace in which you stand…
for One,
both infinite and eternal,
holds all of these
within His hand.

Beauty Hurts

To smell, but not taste... To hear muffled, as through a wall, faint echoes, dying away to cold silence. To see pale reflections in a broken, dirty glass; to perceive yet not touch what was meant to be when the golden light of Heaven first fell upon the silver mists of a newborn Earth... and molten jewels sang in the evening and morning skies.

Faint remembrances of a glory nearly forgotten tears at the hearts of Adam's sons. Shadows only... an uncertain memory, like a lullaby your mother once sang. Paradise lost, now lying somewhere distant beyond the horizon.

An ancient glory now hides somewhere beyond the veil of time. When time shall at last die away, having run its full course, then... oh, then the glory shall live again! But what agony to be now so in-between; to smell, but not taste... to hear only echoes... to yearn for, but not grasp.

The Bleeding Sky

The bleeding sky rains down grace, soothing my grief at once again failing to live up to what I know I should be. Desiring God's spite, for I know it would be just --- yet I am crushed under the weight of His mercy. Ever so reluctantly, I yield to a relentless compassion I cannot hope to understand.

And how could I? How could I hope to rise above mortal constraints and grasp the mind... the heart of He who framed a cosmos so vast, yet holds it in the palm of His hand like a seed? He who dwells in a place beyond space simply cannot fit within the limits of human reasoning. And yet I cannot help but try to understand. So I look up from my small island of time, marooned on a tiny speck adrift in the endless sea of eternity; a place called mortality, where time is strangely constrained to one direction. I try to comprehend the heart and mind of One who, like a Mobius strip, has no beginning or end.

And then --- perhaps that is the key. I am but a poor actor on a rented stage, but the author and the architect sees the end from the beginning. I see but single frayed threads, but He knows the tapestry. Perhaps, just perhaps, I shall find the strength to relinquish my selfish hold on shame and rise up to try once more.

The Bridegroom's Call

Shrouded, I wander alone, probing the silence and shadows of meadow and wood. A whisper above draws my gaze and I turn to study the void across the blackened sea. A trillion worlds staring back... What am I to Thee?

My eyes return to dust and mud, and smaller still I feel. Time claims all deeds and covers them up... whether treacherous or grand. Even the mighty Gibraltar, in time, will wear away to sand.

And yet I've heard, and may believe, that a timeless time is coming. From somewhere beyond the void - or just behind a door - it approaches. A sound will summon it. A trumpet's cry... a bridegroom's shout... and all that is now, all that we think to be real, will simply dissolve. A new reality, an imperishable creation will take hold. Grief and regret fully unknown, every hope and joy and pleasure shall at long last find its fullest expression. And time, having vanished away, will have no power to quench the fires of love.

Chains

A love eternal, unsearchably vast… a passion divine, spilling itself with abandon upon tiny creatures who crawl around a pale blue-green ball, addicted to sorrow--- the shackles of grief and confusion, their dearest friends. The chains of shame, which tear the soul, keep their heads bowed low, embracing the dust and filth… spending their full measure of affection on that which enslaves and consumes.

Finally, love can bear no more. He who is above all, who holds all of creation within His hand, spends the last desperate measure of devotion. The author of eternity steps down into time, enfolding Himself into the very form and appearance of fallen man. Radiance and power which would shame a billion suns hides itself behind a veil of flesh, invading the darkened land. Now face to face with the very object of His love, that veil is torn and light breaks free. Chains dissolve; darkness flees.

Counting Sand

I try to probe the mind of God;
to see all of the whys
and comprehend the how
and catch a glimpse of when.
My mind of flesh, a prisoner of time,
reaches with all of its reason
to see beyond what came before…
I stretch with all of my being
to grasp the eons past;
beyond the beginning,
when the all-in-all
was all there was…
trying to understand
what limitless really means.
To be without end I may just comprehend,
but how can one be… without beginning?
Questions unanswered; I guess they'll never be…
I might just as well sit on the beach
counting sand.

The Darkened Way

We claim to know that God is kind
and loving and merciful and just...
But few and rare indeed
are those who will step out
into the unknown path,
unless they truly must.
We want to know
and see and plan
and design and scheme---
but the kind and loving God
often hides His ways
from prying eyes and anxious hearts,
for truth be told, without the darkness,
we would never learn to trust.

Dreaming of Spring

I find myself waiting in melancholy solitude…
swept into that empty in-between
and making due on memories, like November crows.
The harvest is past, and where is spring?
The whole earth speaks of endings,
a brown, cold stillness
without the joy that snow might bring.
Stillness and waiting…
living on memories
and dreaming of spring.

The Gift Giver

He planted a tree in the barren wilderness and nourished it with life-giving showers. Deep within the secret places of the earth He formed the iron, and gave men the knowledge and skill to refine and forge it, and to cast it into the heavy mallet and fierce, flesh-rending spikes. The thorny bush which was hastily crafted into a regal mockery grew in some forgotten corner of a courtyard by His command and sovereign care. The star which heralded His birth and the darkened, bloody moon which grieved His death... before the breath of life ever entered Adam's lungs, the sovereign Lord set them in their places in the heavens with clockwork precision. And when He climbed that barren and bloody hill on that fateful day, His life was surely not taken from Him;
He gave it away.

The Intrusion

The finite
could never grasp
the infinite
and time
with eternity...
would never catch up
but He who spoke all realms into being

constricted Himself

and stepped into ours,
so that the mortal
might cast off their grave clothes
and lay hold
of life.

Life

Life… real life is a hay field, yielding to God's breath. It is not found in those harder things: concrete, and plaster, and asphalt… vain attempts at significance and permanency which without fail pass away in but a few seasons, victims of a softer hand.

Real life, everlasting life is found in that which bends and bows, and dances and dies, and rises with the breeze once more. It is in that simplicity which hides a billion details, ever changing, yet eternal… birth, death, and renewal, created and sustained by a master hand.

The Knowing

Wisdom is bought
in quiet moments
when self dissolves
and becomes absorbed
by a higher realm.

Solitude begets a knowing
unmatched by scholarly gain.
Hours invested
in focused repose
are never spent in vain.

Mystery

Though the sky be dark, still I cling to your awesome name. I plead of thee, king and lord of all; glorify thyself through this frail frame. I lift and lift and lift my hands, longing to embrace. Still you, oh Lord, oh mighty one of Heaven, must stoop low to receive my praise.

Singing, shouting, and spilling forth rivers of anthem sweet, I raise my voice in tumult to thee, still muster no more than a trickle at your feet. Yet low you bend, down to your knee, drinking deep my love. In mystery so grand, so vast, so deep, infinity embraces the finite, leaving throne above. Leaving glorious dominion, dark captives to free… spilling into the night with holy vengeance, that dark captives might shine as thee.

Private Pain

There is a hell that God alone
shall ever know---
a bitter thorn piercing His heart,
an everlasting sorrow.

He framed the worlds of purest love
and filled the void with light.
He spoke His love and fashioned man
and in him took delight.

And when man strayed and wandered far,
forgiveness was at hand.
The loving Father became Redeemer;
the Creator became a man.

For sin-sick millions He gave His life
and freely offers grace,
yet countless millions prefer their pride
and spit in His face.

Throughout the span
of timeless eternity
one shadow shall remain,
the savage anguish
of love refused---
the Savior's private pain.

Victory and Vengeance

Innumerable warriors, invisible to most, watch in horror as the mightiest of all surrenders willingly to the lash. Foolish men look on, amused… mocking the sacrifice. Still, perhaps pity shall be found at last.

"Barabbas! Barabbas!" Though perplexed, a washing of hands betrays justice, surrendering to the mob's demands. It seems that more blood shall be shed this day.

Carrying the loathsome beam, the shattered and torn frame of a carpenter limps on over rough stone paths. Though in mind-numbing agony, it is rumored that a smile crosses His face. Renewed focus fills His bloodied eyes and He is heard to whisper, "Victory!"

Reclining, He stretches out his hands. Angels cry tears of rage as iron pierces flesh and ignorant men spit in the face of God.

"Vengeance! Vengeance!" the angels scream as all of hell pours into His bosom, there to be consumed.

Small Wonders

Clothed in majesty and fierce might, He dwells in the unbounded expanse beyond mortal constraints of time and space. Inapproachable light, greater than the sum of every star which burns in the deepest heavens, blazes out from the core of His being. By His sheer will were those heavens formed; "Let there be..." and it came to pass. Every grand wonder that has ever met human eyes, and those never yet seen, are but dim, vaporous shadows... reflections of grander things above. There, in the realm of the spirituals, reality is truly real. "Oh, what is man, that You are mindful of him?" Wretched, puny man... so frail and fallen from the grand design... Why should He consider mere dust?

And yet, He who measured out the seas in the palm of His hand crafted the atoms of which those waters are made. A limitless God in childlike delight chose the colors for each wildflower and dabbled the spots on the ladybug. He paints the morning and evening skies and scatters the clouds above; a limitless God, enraptured by limitless love. Though He stands above all and His voice in majesty thunders, yet this limitless God of limitless love delights in small wonders.

Dancing on Mars

As the day's last glimmer of twilight is swallowed by the western sky, I wander the meadow and new wonders meet my waiting eye. A thousand, million distant worlds shine down on me, inviting the bold to step out into the void. Although I am willing, gravity is yet my master and dampens the adventure that might be.

That despair of yearning carries within it a grain of hope... a whisper... the shadow of a joy I will one day know. Gravity will let loose and no longer hold this mortal frame; for what is now mortal, shall no longer be. I will step beyond the black horizon and dance upon the sands of Mars.

Then, I will dive through Jupiter and past Saturn's rings. All of God's wonders shall be laid bare before me; a buffet of delights each passing moment shall bring. And after I explore for a millennia or more, I'll wheel around and blaze a trail home. But first one last stop on my way home from the stars; I'll pause and enjoy a sunset and dance once more on Mars.

The Dirt-Simple Bible

God made man: *"…so God made man in His own image; in the image of God he created him; male and female He created them."* **Genesis 1:27**

Man screwed things up: *"There is none righteous, not one…for all have sinned and fallen short of the glory of God."* **Romans 3:10, 23**

God fixed it: *"…for God so loved the **world** that He **gave His** only begotten Son, that whoever believes in Him should not perish, but have everlasting life."* **John 3:16**

"But He was wounded for our transgressions, He was bruised for our iniquities; the chastisement for our peace was upon Him, and by His stripes we are healed. All we like sheep have gone astray; we have turned, every way, to his own way; and the Lord has laid on Him the iniquity of us all." **Isaiah 53:5-6**

How do I get in on this? *"…if you confess with your mouth the lord Jesus and believe in your heart that God has raised Him from the dead, you will be saved… for 'whoever calls on the name of the Lord shall be saved."* **Romans 10:9, 13**

"He who covers his sins shall not prosper, but whoever confesses and forsakes them shall have mercy." **Proverbs 28:13**

All proceeds benefit **YWAM Faith Harvest Helpers**, a vital and growing ministry of Youth With A Mission, feeding hungry families and providing hope and healing across the United States and around the world. See our website at **www.ywamfhhwa.org** or find us on Facebook. We are located at 12643 Case Road SW, Olympia, WA, 98512. Additional contact information available at the website.

YWAM faith Harvest Helpers, Sharing food and giving hope.

Other titles by Michael M. Middleton

Sacred Journeys

Modern Musings

The Great Deep, revised edition

Whispers of the Divine

Shadows and Substance

Sketches and Reflections

Waves of Glory

Daily Grace (volumes one – four)

Get Real, the pitfall of a cultural Christianity

On Guard, ministering Christ in a messed up world

Castles in the Sky and other tales

The Duck Who Lost His Way

and by Sharon Middleton:

On Winds of Change

Made in the USA
Middletown, DE
23 April 2021